AF654325

CRESCENT PUBLISHING HOUSE

PRESENTS

The Unheard Voice

Embracing Challenges, Cultivating Resilience, and Unfolding the Journey of Muslim Women

The Unheard Voice

Embracing Challenges, Cultivating Resilience, and Unfolding the Journey of Muslim Women

By

Rashida Kouser

CRESCENT PUBLISHING HOUSE

COPYRIGHT

used fictitiously. Any resemblance to actual persons, living or dead, events, or locales is purely coincidental.

First edition

Printed in India

Publication: Crescent Publishing House

ISBN : 978-93-6303-197-5

Price : 299.

ISBN 978-93-6303-197-5

US$ 10.00

51000 >

9 789363 031975

Acknowledgment

All praise and gratitude are owed to Allah (SWT), the Most Compassionate and the Absolute Source of strength, wisdom, and direction. Without His divine decree and boundless mercy, this endeavor would never have taken shape. I extend my heartfelt appreciation to my parents—particularly my resilient mother—who, despite enduring countless hardships, gave me life and nurtured me with unconditional love and perseverance. Her silent sacrifices and unwavering faith laid the foundation for every milestone I've achieved. I am also deeply grateful to my entire family, each of whom— through presence or absence—played a role in shaping my evolution. To every teacher who enlightened me, every friend who stood beside me, and even to those opponents who doubted, challenged, or dismissed my worth—I thank you. Especially those who gave me the toughest trials and the most excruciating experiences; you became unintentional mentors. Your cruelty became the forge that strengthened my spirit, and your rejection gave birth to my resilience. It is through this complex mosaic of blessings and hardships that I found the courage to share my voice. This book stands as a testament to that journey—and to every soul who walks a path of struggle with dignity.

Contents

CHAPTER ONE

The Journey to a Voice

I one day, I would take on the responsibility of articulating the never envisioned myself as an author, nor did I anticipate that silent struggles of countless women. Yet, some paths are not chosen; they unfold before us, shaped by experiences too profound to ignore. My journey into writing was not driven by ambition but by an unshakable urge to bring forth voices that have long remained in the shadows.

From as early as I can remember—perhaps as young as two or three—I was acutely aware of the world around me. Though an introverted child, I absorbed everything—the spoken and the unspoken, the joys and the quiet griefs that lingered in the air.

Among the earliest imprints on my memory was a painful truth: the birth of a girl was seldom a cause for celebration.

I have witnessed it since childhood—the subtle drop in expressions, the hesitant smiles, the whispered condolences masked as empty. A daughter's arrival was met with silence, with sighs, with prayers that the next child would be a son. In contrast, the birth of a boy was an occasion of festivity, of pride, of sweets distributed as though a victory had been secured. Even before a girl could take her first breath, the weight of societal disappointment was already placed upon her shoulders.

I was born in Lolab Khurhama, a place where women's voices often dissolve before they are heard. However, life granted me the opportunity to witness both rural and urban realities, exposing me to the deeply ingrained yet unspoken struggles of women across different landscapes. As I grew, my awareness expanded beyond my surroundings. I studied, listened, and explored the narratives of women globally—their battles, their resilience, and their contributions that remained unrecognized. The pattern was undeniable: whether in villages or cities, in the East or the West, women bore the weight of expectations, restrictions, and sacrifices that the world had learned to accept as natural.

It is essential to clarify—this book is not an anthem of feminism that seeks to diminish the role of men, nor is it a denial of their struggles. Men, too, carry burdens, face betrayals, and navigate societal pressures that often go unspoken. They, too, are victims of expectations—forced into roles of providers, protectors, and decision-makers, sometimes at the cost of their own well-being. I do not wish to undermine their contributions, their sacrifices, or their importance in our lives. Alhamdulillah, men are a blessing, and their presence is integral to the balance of society.

Yet, this book is dedicated to the countless women who never receive the chance to speak for themselves—to those whose voices are subdued before they even dare to rise. It is an attempt to give words to their silent endurance; to illuminate the battles they fight behind closed doors, and to acknowledge their unwavering strength that often goes unnoticed.

A Woman's Worth: Acknowledged in Effort, Forgotten in Existence

Across generations, women have been the silent architects of society, nurturing families, preserving traditions, and fueling progress in every domain. Yet, their sacrifices are absorbed into normalcy, their strength mistaken for duty, their worth measured against standards that fail to recognize their depth.

This book is not merely an exploration of these realities; it is an assertion—a declaration that women's voices matter, that their struggles deserve recognition, and that their contributions must no longer be diminished into footnotes of history.

I have often pondered: Where does a woman truly belong?

Since childhood, I have heard the same refrain echoed in countless households:

"A daughter is only a guest in her parents' home—her real place is in another's house."

This belief, deeply rooted in our society, shapes the way girls are perceived from birth. A son is an investment; a daughter is an expenditure. I have witnessed how people hesitate to invest in a girl's education, health, or personal growth—after all, she is destined to leave. Her autonomy, her self-worth, even her nourishment, is often rationed because, in the end, her future is not considered her own.

I was my parents' third daughter—fortunate to have been nurtured, educated, and valued. But no matter how enlightened a family may be, the biases ingrained in our society run deep. They flow in our veins, shaping expectations and limitations, dictating what a girl should accept as her fate.

For years, I believed—like so many others—that a woman's true home was the one she built with her husband, a place of comfort, protection, and belonging. But life is relentless in its lessons. As I matured, witnessed stories unfold, and encountered the brutal realities of domestic violence, divorce, and honor killings, I came to a painful realization:

A woman does not belong there either.

And then came the most haunting question of all: If neither her parents' house nor her husband's home is truly hers, then where does she go?

The Illusion of a Daughter's Farewell

In our society, parents convince themselves that marriage is an act of relief—a transfer of responsibility, a liberation from the supposed burden of a daughter. Yet, I have seen enough to know this is an illusion. A daughter's departure does not free her parents; it only extends their worries in another form.

How many young women have I seen widowed in their prime?

How many have suffered humiliation at the hands of the very husbands they were told to depend on?

How many mothers, once cherished, have been cast aside by the very children they raised?

How many sisters have been betrayed by the brothers they trusted?

How many women, raised like princesses by loving parents, have been reduced to pitiable conditions after their passing?

And yet, the world convinces women that they are the problem—that they are never enough.

Women across the globe, across generations, are burdened with guilt—guilt that is placed upon them by their own families, by their communities, by the very fabric of society that expects everything from them yet offers them nothing in return.

"You are not good enough."

A whisper that turns into a scream, an echo that never fades.

And then, as time unfolded and maturity graced my perspective, Alhamdulillah, Deen illuminated my path—not as a mere inherited identity, but as a conscious awakening. Before that,

I existed within the fold of Islam without truly grasping its essence. I bore the label of a Muslim, yet my faith lacked rhythm, purpose, and profound understanding. The depth of Islamic wisdom eluded me, and I, like many others, had absorbed the distorted narrative that framed religious adherence as restrictive rather than liberating.

Influenced by the ever-pervasive tides of modernity, I found myself drawn to the allure of Westernization, captivated by the transient glamour of trends and societal ideals. The prevailing misconception that a woman who fully embraces Shariah is somehow confined or deprived of freedom had subtly taken root in my mind. Islam had been misrepresented—even vilified—as a system that curtailed female agency rather than one that elevated and dignified it. Regrettably, I had unknowingly subscribed to this flawed perception, failing to question its validity.

But then, the veil of ignorance lifted. I embarked on a journey to seek knowledge, starting with the fundamentals of my faith, and with each step, I unraveled a reality far removed from what I had been conditioned to believe. Islam was not a shackle; it was an emancipation of the highest order. Long before the world's legal systems even acknowledged the concept of women's rights, Islam had already established them with divine wisdom. Every command ordained by **ALLAH (SWT)** was not a constraint but a safeguard, woven with layers of profound purpose and unparalleled foresight.

This realization was transformative. It ignited within me an insatiable yearning—not just to live by these truths but to contribute something meaningful to the world. A deep conviction took hold of me: the desire to leave behind a legacy that would outlast my existence, something that would serve as Sadaqah Jariyah—a perpetual source of reward and enlightenment. What greater legacy could there be than knowledge? Knowledge that would empower, guide, and inspire not only my children but generations to come.

This book, therefore, is not just an assemblage of words; it is a testament to that awakening. It is a voice for the unheard, a challenge to the misconceptions that distort the truth, and a declaration that a woman's worth is not determined by societal constructs but by the honor and dignity that her Creator has bestowed upon her. Through this work, I seek to reclaim the narrative, to remind the world that Muslim women are not silent spectators in history—they are architects of change, bearers of wisdom, and embodiments of strength.

A woman's struggles do not define her; her resilience does. Yet, how often is her endurance acknowledged? How frequently does the world pause to recognize the weight she carries in silence? Society has conditioned women to suppress their pain, to wipe away their tears before they are seen, to endure without complaint. It has trained them to slim their lips, imprison their tongue, conceal their wounds, and diminish their worth—as if their very existence is an apology they must continuously offer.

But the truth is far from what they have been led to believe. A woman is neither weak nor incomplete. She is not a burden, nor is she meant to shrink herself into spaces that barely accommodate her presence. **ALLAH (SWT)** has honored her, elevated her, and bestowed upon her a role so profound that no worldly oppression can strip it away. Her existence is not defined by societal expectations but by divine wisdom—by the purpose and strength woven into her very being.

For too long, misconceptions—both cultural and external—have distorted the image of Muslim women. Some believe she is oppressed, while others see her as powerless. But to those who truly understand Islam, she is neither. She is a woman who walks with dignity, speaks with wisdom, and upholds values that transcend time. She is the backbone of society, the nurturer of generations, and the silent force behind countless victories—yet, her sacrifices are often dismissed as mere duty.

This discussion is not limited to women alone. Men must be part of this dialogue, not as adversaries but as allies. A father, a brother, a husband, or a son cannot fully understand the depth of a woman's struggles until he listens, learns, and acknowledges the burdens she silently carries. Only through awareness and understanding can they fulfill their roles—not as passive observers, but as active protectors of the rights and dignity that **ALLAH (SWT)** Himself has ordained for women.

This is not about division but about recognition, respect, and reformation. It is about confronting deep-seated gender biases, challenging narratives that strip women of their worth, and fostering a world where a woman does not have to justify her existence—

where she can embrace her role with confidence, knowing that her value is not for society to define but for her Creator to uphold.

True change begins when both women and men recognize the divine equilibrium that Islam has established—a balance where neither gender is superior, but both are honored in their unique roles. It is in this realization that dignity is restored, respect is reclaimed, and the whispers of self-doubt are silenced forever.

The True Faces Behind Closed Doors

Behind every locked door is a woman who has learned to suffer in silence. Society calls her patient, strong, and resilient—but in reality, she has been forced into endurance, not because she is weak, but because she has never been given another choice.

There is the woman who was forced into marriage at a young age, her dreams of education shattered overnight. No one asked if she was ready, if she wanted to marry, or if she had aspirations beyond the walls of her home. Her life was decided for her, and she was expected to accept it without resistance.

There is the mother who has spent her entire life nurturing a family, only to be discarded in her old age, her presence seen as a burden rather than a blessing. She was once the backbone of her household, yet now she sits alone, her sacrifices forgotten.

There is the wife who has endured years of abuse, humiliation, and betrayal, only to be told that divorce is her punishment for aging. She was once cherished, but now, as youth fades, she is considered replaceable.

There is the working woman who wakes before dawn, works tirelessly, and returns home to another shift of unpaid labor. She provides, she sacrifices, yet she is still expected to fulfill all domestic duties without complaint. No one acknowledges her exhaustion. No one thanks her for holding everything together.

There is the unmarried woman who has spent years struggling to meet the expectations of a dowry, watching time slip away while society whispers behind her back. They blame her, not the customs that have reduced marriage to a financial transaction rather than a sacred bond.

These women are everywhere, yet they remain invisible. Their struggles are dismissed as normal, their pain ignored, their worth reduced to their ability to endure.

I refuse to accept that this is the fate of women. I refuse to let their stories remain unheard. This book is my rebellion—my refusal to let silence win.

If a woman is forced into marriage against her will, it is not just a tragedy—it is a crime. If a woman is cast aside after years of sacrifice, it is not just unfortunate—it is an injustice. If a woman spends her life being treated as less than she deserves, it is not just a sad reality—it is a violation of her rights.

For too long, society has expected women to suffer without complaint, to accept oppression as their destiny, to believe that their pain is simply part of being female. This must end.

Every woman deserves respect, dignity, and the freedom to make choices about her own life. She should be valued—not for how much she can endure, but for who she is.

This is not just a book. It is a movement. A testament to the struggles and strength of women who have lived in the shadows for too long.

To every woman who has been forced into silence: I see you. I hear you. And I will not stop speaking until the world listens.

To the society that continues to justify oppression: This book is your mirror. Look at the pain you have normalized. Look at the lives you have ruined with customs that serve no purpose but control.

To those who believe change is impossible: History has proven otherwise. Every movement begins with a voice. This book is mine. And I hope, one day, it becomes yours too.

Writing this book was not a sudden decision—it was a journey shaped by years of personal experiences, research, and reflection.

During my doctorate, I focused o**n The Emancipation of Women: A Case Study of District Kupwara**, a research topic that opened my eyes to the struggles of women beyond my immediate surroundings. My academic journey exposed me to gender issues on both global and regional levels, allowing me to study the deeply ingrained challenges women face across cultures. Through extensive research, literature reviews, and field studies, I gained a profound understanding of the systemic oppression, inequality, and societal expectations that shape women's lives.

But my doctoral research was not the only factor that pushed me to write this book—it was just one part of a larger awakening. As I explored the struggles of women, I also began to notice the injustices within my own community, my own household, and even within myself. Each experience, each story I encountered, solidified my determination to write.

I had already published my first book, **Inspirational Thoughts and Words of Wisdom**, a collection of poetry addressing social issues. However, life took an unexpected turn when the COVID-19 pandemic disrupted my research, forcing me to put my doctorate on hold. Around the same time, I got engaged, then married, and soon found myself navigating the overwhelming realities of pregnancy and motherhood.

Both my pregnancies were so complicated and challenging and required complete rest due to complications, making it impossible for me to continue my doctorate. Motherhood became my full-time commitment, and as a deeply protective mother, I could not entrust my children's care to anyone else. My life revolved around them, and for a time, my ambitions were set aside.

Yet, the fire to write never truly left me. There were nights when I lay awake, restless, feeling the weight of the stories left untold. Balancing two toddlers while trying to carve out time for writing was an overwhelming struggle, but I knew I had to do it.

Writing was not just a passion—it was my calling, my responsibility.

Somehow, through all the extra just words on paper; it is a reflection of my journey, my struggles, my observations, and most importantly, my unwavering belief that change is possible.

The time has come to tell these stories, to break the silence, and to demand a better future for women everywhere.

CHAPTER TWO

Centuries of Struggle Women Confronting Discrimination and Inequality

As per the Holy Qur'an and Islamic teachings the word "women"(نساء) holds significant meaning and encompasses various aspects of life, rights and responsibilities. The Holy Quran states that men and women are created from a single soul, emphasizing their inherent equality. ***Surah (An- Nisa) [4:1] say's "O mankind, fear your Lord, Who created you from one soul and creates from it it's mate and dispersed from both of them many men and women and fear*** **ALLAH (SWT)** ***through Whom you ask one another, and the wombs. indeed,*** **ALLAH (SWT)** ***is ever, over you an observer.***

The origin of the word women traces back to old English and Proto - Germanic roots. The word "women" derives from the old English word "Wi-fmann", which is a compound of "Wif" (women wife) and "man" (person, human being. Over time, the term, evolved, with "wi`fmann" becoming, "wimmann" & later women in Middle
East.

In Islamic teachings particularly in the Quran & Islamic Tradition, the word "women" or "Nisa" (نساء) carries profound significance, both of in terms of its linguistic origin & it's religious context.

Etymology: - The Arabic word **(**نساء**) is** derived from the root word (Niswah) which refer to women or females. "**ALLAH (SWT)** created women from the rib of Adam so that she may be a source of tranquility for him". The existence of women infused new life into the soul and body of man, initiating the beginning of the human lineage on earth.

"**ALLAH (SWT)** created women as a living embodiment of modesty, beauty, and love so that women in this world can discern their inherent purpose and role and emerged as catalysts of respect, Solace knowledge & prosperity of society. Nature has distinctly shaped men and women, yet it has not rendered women weak".

However, as the human population expanded across the world, people' perspectives & inclinations towards various aspect's began to diverge. Human ignorance and avarice have significantly diminished the stature of women. In Islam women's life ought to resemble that of a sovereign, presiding over her household where she discharged her responsibilities while being endowed with dignity, reverence & protection.

In ancient societies worldwide women faced significant deprivation of their basic rights. They were systematically excluded from full participation in social, political and religious activities unlike their male counterparts. Access to higher education was largely reserved for boys, leaving girls with limited opportunities for intellectual and professional advancement. In addition, women were often denied their rightful share of property and inheritance reinforcing their subordinate status within their communities and families. These historical perspectives underscore the pervasive gender inequalities that shaped ancient societies globally. In ancient Arabia women were egregiously marginalized, lacking access to fundamental rights. They were systematically denied opportunities for higher education and marriages were frequently imposed upon them against their will. Shockingly in certain tribes, female infants were subjected to live burial deemed to be a burdensome liability; widows faced stringent restrictions against remarriage enduring profound hardships as a result.

The narrative of women's oppression span's centuries. Women's voices have been systematically suppressed for generation and even in the 21st century concerted efforts continue to stifle their advocacy for their rights. If we discuss about the contemporary era, often referred to as the 21st century, it would not be erroneous to assert that women remain deprived of their rights and continue to endure oppression & exploitation. There is no doubt that the current era, bolstered by advancements in technology and science affords considerable convenience for women. However, it is undeniable that contemporary women are subjected to such overwhelming social pressures that they have often lost sight of their life's purpose & identity.

The foremost objective of human existence is to worship **ALLAH (SWT)**. Beyond this, **ALLAH (SWT)** has designated distinct roles for men & women. **ALLAH (SWT)** did not create men and women as equal but different and endowed them with distinct roles. **ALLAH (SWT)** granted men a degree of superiority over women, appointing them as guardians & providers due to their financial and other responsibilities towards women. ***Surah An-Nisa (4:34)***

"Men are the protectors and maintainers of women because* ALLAH (SWT) *has given them responsibility over them and because they spend from their wealth on them."

ALLAH (SWT) exempted women from the duty of earning a livelihood, enabling them to concentrate on the upbringing of the next generation & to transform the home into a sanctuary of serenity through their devotion, diligence & affection.

In the 21st century, women around the world continue to face discrimination and inequality in various aspects of their lives. Despite significant progress in women's rights & gender equality, the modern era presents new and enduring challenges. From the workplace to the home, in politics, education, & beyond, women encounter barriers that hinder their full participation & advancement. This exploration delves into the Multifaceted issues of gender discrimination faced by Muslim women, shedding light on the personal stories & systematic structure that perpetuate inequality. In Today's world, where there is a pronounced emphasis on gender parity and numerous initiatives are being instituted to guarantee women their full rights, & where legislation is being enacted to secure women's entitlement.

Conversely, we still witness numerous instances of systematic oppression and egregious injustices against women while societal progress is evident, there remains a substantial amount of work to be done to ensure that women receive the respect, dignity, protection and comprehensive rights to which they are entitled. With the advent of Islam women were bestowed with a transformative societal identity and Sharia law endowed them with empowerment and dignity. Under Sharia, women are granted reverence, honor and robust protection in every relationship. In Islam, women are absolved from the obligations of financial provision, which are exclusively assigned to men. Consequently, men are accorded a degree of precedence over women. A man is entrusted with the responsibility of providing for a woman, ensuring her safety, and offering her protection, whether he is her father, son, brother or husband. This obligation has been divinely bestowed upon him by **ALLAH (SWT).** When **ALLAH (SWT)** has bestowed such a high status upon women, why does the world continue to marginalize them? Even today, people attempt to deprive women of their rightful happiness. Differentiation is still made between the birth of a daughter and that of a son. It is not just the ignorant; even in educated and affluent families, boys are given preferences.

ALLAH (SWT) has endowed women with authority, but due to societal ignorance & women's lack of self- assurance, society has usurped their rights.

When examining inheritance rights in Islam, it becomes evident that the religion allocates shares for women in every familial relationship. A Muslim woman is entitled to her rightful shares as a mother, sister, wife and daughter, in accordance with the Qur'an and the sunnah. When considering govt- enacted laws, women are entitled to inheritance rights in every country. However, in Society, we often observe that women are deprived of their rightful shares of inheritance. Only a small portion of women eventually receive their inheritance entitlements.

Regularly, we observe inheritance disputes, involving women in the. Often, these cases see daughters challenging their parents, sisters contesting their brothers or wives opposing their husbands. Current circumstances and events reveal that, even in the 21st century, women remain victims of oppression and injustice, thereby being deprived of their rightful entitlements.

Now let's discuss forced marriages. In Islam, marriage is a sacred and pure bond, ordained by **ALLAH (SWT)** to be a source of tranquility and comfort for both men and women. It serves as a means for nurturing and advancing future generations. Forced marriage is a union where one or both parties are married without their consent. Islam places a strong emphasis on consent and mutual agreement in marriage. The Holy Quran explicitly states" ***O you who have believed, it is not lawful for you to inherit women by compulsion." (Qur'an 4:19)*** highlighting that forced marriage is not permissible. The Hadiths, or sayings of the prophet Mohammad states, ***"The widow and the divorced women shall not be married until her order is obtained," [Sahih Bukhari 5138]***

Nonetheless we frequently observe in our congregations that women are often deprived of their rightful entitlements in matters of marriage. Generally, in our society decisions regarding marriage are often made by me. We frequently observe in our society that consulting women about their own marriage is often deemed unnecessary. Due to such coercion, girls often resort to suicide or decide to flee their homes, there by leaving an indelible stain on their own their family's reputation.

Dowry demands:

In Islam, the concept of dowry, referred to as **(Mahr)** is a fundamental and important aspect of marriage "**Mahr"** is a mandatory gift given by the groom to the bride at the time of marriage. It is a symbol of respect, responsibility and commitment towards the bride ensuring her financial security and dignity within the marriage.

The requirements of Mahr are explicitly stated in the Qur'an **ALLAH (SWT)** command' in ***Surah An- Nisa (4:4) "And give the women (upon marriage) their bridal gifts previously."***

Mahr can take various forms depending on the agreement between the bride and groom. It can be in the form of (Monetary) cash on financial assets, property, land houses etc. jewellery gold silver etc.

However, we perceive in - laws within our society tyrannical. One significant factor is that the superfluous & ostentatious traditions prevalent in our culture have rendered marriage exceedingly challenging & expensive. Moreover, under the pretext of tradition, the bride's family is extorted and subjected to injustices by the in - laws which constitute a profound embarrassment for our society. In our society unfounded and frivolous customs are frequently observed. Despite the prohibition of gold adornment for men in Islam, there remains a tradition where the bride's family ceremoniously bestows gold upon the groom, ultimately this possession gold becomes the possession of the groom's family. If affluent individuals engage in such custom's, it would not pose a significant issue. However, our society is plagued by a culture of imitation, causing these traditions to become burdensome for the average person. Consequently, marriage (Nikkah) has become prohibitively expensive fornication and immoral relationships have become more accessible and affordable. As a result, unlimited women surpass the marriageable age each year due to these customs and traditions. In contemporary times dowry has been rendered so indispensable for the bride's parents that it imposes an immense burden on an impoverished father, leaving him financially crippled and unable to repay the debt, even after exhausting all his resources.

If we consider our Kashmiri culture, the bride's family incurs expenses running into lakhs solely for the groom's reception. Moreover, there are customs that require the bride's family to present gifts to the groom's family, and it is also tradition to give gold ornaments to the groom's family members. As a result, the bride's family endures substantial hardship to arrange the marriage. Even after parting with their cherished daughter, they find that the insatiable greed & avarice of others remain unabated.

A father invests his life's savings in his daughter's marriage, hoping that once she gets married, he will be relieved of his responsibilities. However, the situations have deteriorated so severely that the bride's family is expected to cover all expenses including the hospital bills even at the time of delivery. Despite enduring such considerable hardship, there is no assurance of how the bride's future will, unfold fare in her in- laws household. If we consider that dowry, an entrenched social and religious anomaly, has become so deeply ingrained in our society that in the current circumstances, it has become an interminable practice.

Divorce & Custody Rights

The exploitation of Muslim women in matters of divorces & custody is a complex issue, deeply rooted cultural, legal and societal norm' s. Addressing these challenges requires a multifaceted approach including legal reforms, community education, & support system that empower women to exercise their rights fully & fairly. In many Muslim communities, divorce and custody issues present significant challenges for women. Despite the principles of fairness & justice enshrined in Islamic cultural practices & legal framework often leave women vulnerable to exploitation & injustice.

Divorce, known as [**Talaq**] in Islamic terminology, is a significant yet sensitive subject within the Muslim community. While Islam provides clear guidelines on the processes & guidelines of divorce, the actual practice often diverges due to cultural, legal & social factors. In Islam divorce is permitted but considered a lawful act that is profoundly abhorred by Allah. In Islam, the importance of nurturing relationships is emphasized, and marriage is to be sustained with love, compassion, patience, and gratitude. However, there are instances where marital issues arise, making life increasingly challenging. Thus, due to such issues, divorce between husband & wife may become unnecessary. However, it is frequently observed in our Societies that the right to initiate divorce is exclusively vested in the husband. Conversely, Islam affords women the option of **(Khula)** when despite all efforts they find the marriage untenable. In our society, regardless of the extent of a woman's sufferings, there is often undue pressure on her to sustain the marriage at all cost.

Numerous women endure lives marked by abuse, suffering prolonged subjugation by their in-laws and domestic violence, often under the guise of patience. This is frequently attributable to deep seated factors that lead to women being deprived of their rights & autonomy.

Domestic responsibilities

Domestic responsibilities including all house chores, child care and elder care is essential for the smooth functioning of any family. However, these task' often fall disproportionately on women, limiting their opportunities for education, careers & personal development. In the context of Muslim women, these responsibilities are influenced by a blend of religious teachings, cultural traditions and societal norms. Islamic teachings emphasize the importance of mutual respect and cooperation between spouses, advocating for a balanced distribution of household duties. However cultural practices often place the bulk of domestic work in women, creating a huge gap between religious ideas & everyday reality. This dynamic can lead to significant physical and emotional strain, affecting women's overall wellbeing.

Moreover, the expectations placed on women can vary widely across communities and regions. While some women may find support and share responsibilities within their families, others may face rigid gender roles that restrict their participation in public & professional life.

Understanding the diverse experiences of Muslim women is crucial to addressing the unique challenges they face in balancing domestic responsibilities with personal aspirations.

Since childhood I have observed in my community the systematic oppression of women rights with them being unjustly labelled as burdens. My Question to society is if women are deemed burdens than who is that who turns a house into a home. If women are deemed burdens, then let men carry their own burden for nine months and give birth to themselves. The one who gives birth is labeled as a burden. The wife who leaves her own home to settle with a strange person is also called a burden. The sister who quietly forfeits her inheritance for her brother, leaving with a stranger without knowing what her future holds, sacrifices her share to preserve her relationship with her brothers, and yet she is still considered a burden. Do the men of our society alone bear the burden & pain of these relationships

In today's progressive Era, where women surpass men in the field of education, numerous women are also now working and earning. We might say they are undertaking dual responsibilities. Despite this, women's contribution remains undervalued. They work alongside men, earning a livelihood, while also bearing the full weight of household duties, child care & education yet, they continue to be considered inferior.

A woman is a vibrant, sentient being, imbued with her own aspirations and desires. Her skills and intelligence enhance her persona, adding a radiant brilliance to her character. **ALLAH (SWT)** has endowed a woman with delicate sensibilities; she is neither a robot nor a machine built to perform all household tasks. **ALLAH (SWT)** has bestowed upon humanity the gift of freedom along with the rights and duties that accompany every relationship, which must be fulfilled with adherence to his divine commands. In our society women are often treated to unpaid servants, compelled to work like laborers. The true extent of this oppression often becomes apparent after marriage. No matter how educated, respectable or from how esteemed a family a woman may be, & regardless of whether she earns equal to or more than a man, she is rarely given the respect & honour she truly deserves. Mostly in our society in - laws often perceive her as nothing more than a domestic helper, assuming she has no personal life and individuality, no commitments. Even if a woman works 24/7 in her in - laws' home, it hardly matters to anyone.

"Our religion is one of ease; **ALLAH (SWT)** does not burden a soul beyond its capacity. Yet, it is people who wrong themselves." ***Qur'an, Surah Al-Baqarah (2:286): "*ALLAH (SWT)* does not burden a soul beyond its capacity."***

Qur'an, Surah Yunus (10:44): "Indeed, **ALLAH (SWT)** ***does not wrong the people at all, but it is the people who wrong themselves."***

ALLAH (SWT) has created mankind free and has bestowed upon its certain responsibilities, particularly concerning relationships. However, in our society, everyone seeks to impose their burdens on others which is why women find themselves in such a predicament. They are neither accorded the respect and status they fully deserve, nor are they granted their due rights. Unfortunately, we cannot deny that women in today's era are still not free from the chains of oppression. In Fact, the modern woman is even more oppressed, and she has lost her true essence by bearing the burden of dual responsibilities.

Neglecting the Nurturer maternal health in crises: -

In *Many* Muslim communities, the role of the mother is revered, celebrated in poetry and praised in religious texts. Islam places immense value in the health and wellbeing if mother's, recognizing their central role in the family & society yet paradoxically, the actual care provided to mother's during pregnancy, childbirth and postpartum is often woefully inadequate. The cultural conundrum the for motherhood is sometimes superficial, manifesting mere in expectations than in support. Cultural norms may demand that a woman bears multiple children, often without adequate gap between pregnancies leads to physical exhaustion & complications combined with the lack of autonomy over reproductive Choices, exacerbates the health risks faced by Muslim women. Access to quality healthcare is a significant issue.in many regions, Muslim women face barriers to receiving adequate maternal care due to poverty, lack of education, insufficient health care infrastructure and mainly due to the negligence of husbands. Rural areas, in particular, are often underserved, with pregnant women having to travel long distances to receive even basic medical attention. Furthermore, the absence of female health care providers in some regions can deter women from seeking care, due to cultural norms around gender interaction.

Mental health: the silent struggle

Maternal health is not limited to physical well-being; mental health is also very crucial & important. Postpartum depression, anxiety and other mental health issues are prevalent but frequently overlooked or stigmatized in many Muslim communities. The lack of awareness and resources for mental health care combined with societal expectations of resilience & self - sacrifice, leaves many women to suffer in silence. The Islamic perspective on mental health is often misunderstood or ignored, despite its emphasis on compassion & the importance of caring for the mind as well as the body. Islamic teachings clearly emphasize the importance of maternal health. The prophet Mohammad (Pbuh) spoke about the women's elevated status in every relationship. However, the lack of connection between the teachings & modern practice is glaring. In some communities there is a gap between the religious ideals & the actual treatment of women, particularly in the context of maternal health.

Addressing the negligence of mental health among Muslim women requires a multi-faceted approach. It involves improving access to health care, educating communities about the importance of maternal health, & breaking down cultural barriers that prevent women from seeking and receiving the care they need. Additionally, there must be a concerted effort to align practice with Islamic teachings, ensuring that the reverence for motherhoods reflected comprehensive, compassionate care. We honor the true spirit of Islam & empower the nurturers of our society. The wellbeing of mother is not just a private concern; it is public duty; a religious obligation is a moral imperative.

Violence and Abuse

Violence and Abuse against women are pervasive issues that transcend cultural, ethnic & religious boundaries. For Muslim women, these challenges are often compounded by societal expectations, cultural practices, & the misuse of religious teachings. Muslim women experience various forms of abuse, including physical violence, emotional manipulation, psychological torment & sexual exploitation. These forms of abuse may occur within the home, perpetrated by spouses or family members or in the broader social settings where Muslim women are marginalized or discriminated against. The insidious nature of such abuse often leaves these women feeling isolated or voiceless, unable to seek help due to fear of stigma or further harm. In our society, instances of violence against women are frequently encountered. Even when a woman raises her voice for her rights, she is often labelled as insolent or uncouth. The mental abuse against a woman often begins in her own home, where she is born.

From a very tender age, girls are frequently instilled with the notion that they are a burden and mere transients in their own homes, fated to depart sooner or later. In our society parents frequently erode a girl's confidence instead of fostering it, causing her to navigate life oblivious to her own intrinsic value, perpetually seeking validation & support from others. As soon as a girl reaches teen age and the prospect of marriage arises, she is often burdened with the same inferiority complex that those who marry her & take her into their home are to be served with unwavering patience & gratitude. Regardless of the circumstances, whether she is respected or not, she is expected to endure with unyielding forbearance. From childhood a girl envisions her wedding day with hopeful dreams, but when she finally leaves for the marital home, she is tragically made to feel that this place, too, does not truly belong to her.

In our society when a woman asserts her rights, her voice is often stifled before it can be heated. And if her efforts persist despite this, she is often met with physical violence in order to suppress her further. Even if the girl wants to get a choice marriage with the consent of her family even then she is subjected to criticism & violence. If a woman endures immense cruelty in her in-law's home, she is still expected to silently bear every issue with patience. The phenomenon of domestic violence within an in-law's household represents a dimension of abuse that often remains obscure by cultural & familial norms. In many societies, the traditional family structure extends beyond the nuclear unit, incorporating in - laws who hold significant influence over daily life. This extended family dynamic can create an environment ripe for abuse, as women navigating these complex relationships may encounter systematic & overt mistreatment. Such abuse can manifest in various forms, including physical violence, emotional manipulation, & psychological coercion, each contributing to the erosion of women's sense of self & security.

Within the in- law household, the boundaries of abuse often become blurred by the interplay of traditional expectations & familial authority. Women are frequently subjected to physical violence not only by their spouses but also by other family members, who may view such actions as permissible within the context of their cultural or social norms. This physical abuse is often accompanied by emotional and psychological torment, where verbal degradation, coercive control & strategic isolation are employed to undermine women's autonomy. The pressure to conform to the rigid family expectations of familial harmony can exacerbate the woman's vulnerability, trapping her in a cycle of abuse & silence. The barriers preventing women from seeking help in these situations are substantial & multifaceted. The stigma associated with reporting domestic abuse particularly within the extended family context, often deters women from coming forward. Fear of social ostracism, familial dishonor, and the potential for escalating violence if the abuse is disclosed contribute to the silence surrounding these issues. Moreover, inadequate legal protections and limited access to support services within tightly- knit communities further entrench women in abusive situations, rendering them both physically and emotionally isolated.

Addressing domestic violence in an in-law's household necessitates a comprehensive and culturally sensitive approach. Effective legal frameworks must be established to protect women from abuse, alongside enhanced support systems that provide accessible resources & intervention services. Public awareness campaigns & community education are also critical in challenging norms & reducing the stigma associated with seeking help. By fostering an environment that supports women's rights and addresses the complexities of familial abuse, society can work toward mitigating these hidden crises & empowering women to reclaim their autonomy. In some households, domestic violence can manifest in troubling way's when a woman is obliged to live with her brother-in-law, who is considered non- mahram according to Islamic guidelines. This arrangement often places the woman in a precarious situation where the lack of clear boundaries & personal privacy can become a breeding ground for harassment and abuse. Living in a joint family with a non- mahram male, especially in a setting where the woman is already vulnerable, can lead to numerous challenges. These include emotional manipulation, and even physical abuse, all of which undermine her sense of security & personal autonomy. The situation is further complicated by societal and familial pressures, which may discourage her from seeking help or leaving the abusive environment.

CHAPTER THREE

Modern Challenges: Addressing The Stereotypes & Challenges Faced by Muslim Women Today

In examining the modern era, we observe that while advancement in technology, artificial intelligence, and science have significantly enhanced human comfort, these developments & the drastic changes in civilizations have also given rise to a global tumult. Muslim women along with people around the world, have found themselves affected by this upheaval. We live in an age defined by social media, where the entire spectrum of the world's imagery is accessible through our mobile phones at any moment and from any location. Since the dawn of creation, as ordained by **ALLAH (SWT),** women have been a perennial subject of controversy. In the current era, social media, the beauty industry, fashion shows, and the allure of Hollywood & Bollywood have transformed women into a major focal point of societal discord. As a result of the restless progression of changing times, A Muslim woman has, regrettably, lost the vision of the fundamental purpose of her existence & identity, becoming increasingly immersed in the prevailing trends of the era. In the contemporary materialistic world, women have become ensnared in an environment where preserving their very existence has grown increasingly challenging. In this age women are compelled to navigate relentless struggles & exert tremendous effort to protect their integrity & preserve their identity. In this era dominated by social media individuals tend to sacrifice their inner peace by incessantly comparing their lives to others. The rise of the makeup industry & professional beauty standards has eroded the societal appreciation for a woman's natural & understated beauty. Nowadays both non - Muslim & Muslim women have become ensnared by the makeup industry, fashion trends & social media. Consequently, it has become increasingly challenging for a modest and dignified woman to maintain tranquility & contentment in today's world.

The Dichotomy of Beauty: - Authenticity Vs Artificiality

In contemporary society, the pursuit of Beauty has evolved into a complex & often troubling phenomenon. As the allure of artificial enhancements, such as plastic surgeries, Botox, lip fillers, contact lenses, hair extensions, Hd airbrush makeup & much more become more prevalent, the value of natural beauty seems to diminish.

These alterations prominently displayed on social media, paint an idealized image that many women are compelled to emulate. This pressure to conform to unrealistic beauty standards not only reshapes societal perceptions but also inflicts significant emotional & psychological strain on those who cannot choose not to partake in this manufactured allure.

The rise of artificial beauty:

In today's world, beauty is increasingly defined by artificial enhancements. Women flock to cosmetic procedures to achieve a desired look often driven by societal pressures & media portrayals. Botox smooths out wrinkles, plastic surgeries reshape physical features, lip fillers enhance volume, contact lenses change eye colour & hair extensions add length & fullness. Simply nothing is impossible in this modern era except defeating death and old age. This pursuit of a perfected appearance has become a hallmark of modern beauty standards. The proliferation of these beauty trends in social media platforms exacerbates the pressure to confirm. Women showcase their enhanced features, perpetuating a cycle where natural beauty is overshadowed by the manufactured ideal. The result is a relentless drive to meet these often-unattainable standards, leading many to experience anxiety, self- doubt, and a distorted self-image.

The Islamic perspective Modesty & Authenticity

In contrast, Muslim women are guided by principles of modesty outlined in their faith. The practice of purdah is not merely a cultural or religious obligation but as a means of preserving one's dignity & focusing on inner qualities rather than external appearance.

For Muslim women, it represents a commitment to **ALLAH (SWT)** and a safeguard for their spiritual wellbeing in the hereafter. This practice is a profound expression of faith, a personal conviction, often understood or undervalued in broader societal contexts.

Social pressure & Mental trauma:

The juxtaposition of these two beauty paradigms - artificial enhancements versus modesty - creates a unique set of challenges for Muslim women. Social media & modern beauty standards exert immense pressure on artificial ideals, while Islamic teachings encourage modesty & authenticity. This conflict can lead to significant mental & emotional trauma. And there are unlimited challenges that Muslim women face.

Social judgement: -

Muslim women who adhere to modesty may face criticism or alienation for not aligning with mainstream beauty standards. The stark contrast between their natural appearance & the prevalent artificial beauty ideals can lead to feelings of inadequacy & exclusion.

Internal conflict: Balancing faith-based practices with societal expectations can create internal conflict & stress. The desire to remain true to religious principles while navigating a world that values superficial beauty can be emotionally tracing.

Marital strain: The societal glorification of artificial beauty can impact personal relationships, particularly within marriages partners influenced by these ideal's may unfairly judge their spouses, leading to strained relationships & emotional distress. The idealization of artificial beauty can result in dissatisfaction with one's partner, causing significant relational & psychological strain.

The impact of Artificial beauty on Marital relationships:

In today's society where artificial beauty is highly praised, there is a growing trend of men becoming attracted to women who embody these enhanced standards. This shift can have detrimental effects on Marital relationships, especially when men hold unrealistic expectations influenced by media portrayals. Wives who embrace natural beauty or modesty may face undue criticism or pressure from their spouses, leading to emotional trauma & relationship discord. Men's preferences for artificially enhanced features can create a disparity between partners, exacerbating feelings of inadequacy & contributing to marital dissatisfaction. This phenomenon not only affects individual self- esteem but also impacts overall health of relationships making it imperative to address these unrealistic expectations & promote a more inclusive understanding of beauty.

The clash between modern ideals of artificial beauty & personal challenges. As the quest for perfection continues to shape beauty standards, it is crucial to recognize and address the emotional & psychological impacts of these trends for Muslim women navigating this landscape involves balancing faith, personal identity, & societal expectations. By fostering a more authentic & inclusive defamation of beauty, we can work towards alleviating the pressures & traumas that arise from these conflicting ideals. In the contemporary era, the pervasive influence of the internet & smart phones has transformed the landscape of human interactions, presenting unique challenges for Muslim women dedicated to upholding modesty & the sanctity of their relationships. The ease with which men can engage in online conservations & casual dating - actions expressly. Forbidden in Islam - has introduced an additional layer of complexity to marital dynamics. The allure of online (Fitna) can erode trust, yet many Muslim women are responding with profound resilience, drawing strength from their faith & the teachings of the Qur'an & Sunnah.

To combat these challenges, modern Muslim women priorities transparent communication within their relationships, reflecting the prophetic tradition that emphasizes the importance of mutual understanding. The Prophet Mohammad () said, "The *best of you are those who are best with their families* (Sunan Ibn Majah). By fostering open dialogues, they establish clear boundaries & expectations about technology use, thereby reinforcing a foundation of trust & respect. This proactive approach not only mitigates the risks of online distractions but also cultivates a supportive environment where both partners feel valued & secure. Moreover, these women recognize the need to nurture the emotional & spiritual dimensions of their marriages, as outlined in Islamic teachings. They strive to create homes infused with the remembrance of **ALLAH (SWT)** (Dhikr) & rooted in the principles of faith. Regular prayer, seeking knowledge & participation in community activities not only fortify their marriages but also act as protective barriers against the moral pitfalls of the digital age. As the Holy Qur'an states, "***And remember*** **ALLAH (SWT)** ***so that you may be successful"*** (62:10), emphasizing the need for constant spiritual engagement.

When faced with the emotional burden of potential infidelity or in appropriate online behavior, many Muslim women turn to prayer (dua) a reflection for guidance. This practice is deeply embedded in the Islam as exemplified by the Prophet's reliance on prayer in times of difficulty. As it is mentioned in holy Qur'an, "O ***you who have believed, seek help through patience & prayer indeed,*** **ALLAH (SWT)** ***is with patient (Surah Baqarah- 153)***

Through spiritual resilience, they seek clarity & wisdom, allowing the teachings of the Qur'an & Hadith to guide their decisions & actions. This commitment to faith empowers them to navigate modern complexities with a sense of purpose and direction. Additionally contemporary Muslim women are increasingly asserting their rights within the framework of Islamic law, understanding that Islam grants the right to protect their dignity & honor. As stated in the Qur'an, "***And among his signs is that he created for you from yourselves mates that you may find tranquility in them." (Qur'an 30:21).***

This understanding compels them to seek justice and support when faced betrayal, whether through counselling involving trusted community leaders, or pursuing legal resources in accordance with Islamic principles. They ensure that their voices are heard advocating for relationship's built on fairness, respect & a mutual commitment to uphold Islamic values. In their pursuit of a harmonious relationship, many Muslim women also turn to the teachings of Prophet Mohammad () who emphasized the importance of compassion and kindness. He advised, "the *most perfect believer is the one who is best in conduct & most kind to his family*" (Sunan Abu Dawood). By embodying these principles, Muslim Women cultivates a nurturing environment that discourages harmful behavior reinforcing the bond of love & respect the is foundational in any marriage. Furthermore, the importance of community support cannot be understated. Muslim women often seek solidarity among their peers, participating in groups or forums where they can share experiences & strategies for navigating modern challenges. These communal ties foster a sense of belonging & provide essential encouragement reinforcing the notion that they are not alone in their struggles engaging with others who share similar values & experiences creates a support network to stand firm against negative influences. The proactive involvement of Muslim women in educating themselves and their families about the potential danger's digital interactions is another crucial aspect of their resilience. They often take the initiative to lead discussions on the importance of safeguarding one's faith in the face of temptation, thereby equipping younger generations with the tools to navigate the complexities of the digital age. By instilling strong moral values & encouraging critical thinking. These women ensure that their children understand the significance of maintaining a virtuous lifestyle, both online and offline.

In summary, today's modest Muslim women are adeptly navigating the challenges of the digital age by drawing on the timeless teachings of the Quran & Sunnah. Their unwavering commitment to faith & integrity not only safeguard their relationships from the dangers of modern temptation's but also exemplifies the strength and grace inherent in living a life dedicated to Allah. By prioritizing open communication, spiritual engagement and community support, they effectively up hold the moral fabric of their families, ensuring that their homes remain sanctuaries of faith, love and mutual respect in an increasingly complex world. Through their actions, they serve as role models for future generations, demonstrating that adherence to Islamic principles can lead to fulfilling and resilient relationship's, even amidst the challenges of contemporary society.

Navigating parenthood: The modern Struggles of Muslim women

In the modern world, Muslim mother's encounter a distinct array of parenting challenges. Their responsibilities transcend the traditional domain's demanding the preservation of religious values amidst secular societal influence, all while managing contemporary pressures. The role of the Muslim mothers has evolved, requiring an exceptional balance of tradition, adaptability, and resilience.

The modern Muslim mother is tasked with safeguarding her children's faith in a world steeped in secular ideologies. Navigating an environment dominated by materialism, consumerism, and shifting moral values, she must ensure her children uphold the principles of Islam, such as prayer, modesty, and ethical behavior, while integrating into a society where these values are often marginalized. This responsibility places immense pressure on the mother, who must become both a guardian of faith and a mediator of two often conflicting worldviews.

The Dual burden of provider a caregiver

The economic demands of modern life frequently necessitate that Muslim women assume dual roles within the family. Not only are they the primary caregivers, but they also contribute financial balancing professional commitments with household duties. This dual responsibility leads to an immense physical and emotional burden, as these mothers must fulfill their obligations in both the public and private spheres without reprieve. The notion of balancing work & family is no longer a choice but a necessity, exacerbating the exhaustion & mental strain they endure.

The challenge of Islamic upbringing is secular school's

The secular educational system presents a formidable challenge for Muslim mothers who are intent on raising their children with strong Islamic values. While secular schools emphasize a broad non - religious curriculum, Muslim mothers must work to instill a sense of faith and cultural identity in their children.

This process requires delicacy, as children must learn to reconcile their religious upbringing with the often-contrasting norms and expectations of their peers and educators. Ensuring that Islamic principles are neither lost nor diminished in this environment is a primary concern for many mother's

Mental Health: The invisible struggle

The mental health struggles of Muslim mother's often go unaddressed of parenting, compounded by societal expectations & the demand of balancing multiple roles, frequently lead to stress, anxiety & burn out. However, the stigma surrounding mental health within many Muslim communities prevents these mothers from seeking the help they need. Mental health is often perceived through faith, with struggles seen as a personal failing or a lack of religious devotion, rather than as legitimate concern requiring attention & care. This perception further silences mothers who are already bearing a heavy emotional load. The modern challenges faced by Muslim mothers in their parenting journey are profound & multifaceted. The task of preserving faith while navigating a secular world, managing dual responsibilities & confronting stereotypes, all while contending with the erosion of traditional support structures, demands remarkable strength & resilience. Despite these Obstacles, Muslim mothers continue to rise to the occasion nurturing a new generation that is rooted in faith, equipped to engage with the world, & proud of their identity.

Their perseverance is a testament to the enduring power of motherhood in Islam & the vital role they play in shaping the future of their families & communities. In the materialistic world we live in today, where wealth and status have become measures of success, Muslim women often face overwhelming economic pressure to contribute financially to their household. Many enter the workforce not out of personal desire, but out of necessity, in order to sustain their families, financial stability and maintain social standing. The burden of this responsibility, however, often comes at a high cost particularly to the upbringing of their children. As their women strive to balance their professional duties with their roles a mother's, they often mind themselves stretched thin, unable to devote the time and attention necessary to nurture their children's moral and emotional development. The guilt of missing out on their children's formative years of being absent from their daily lives, weighs heavily on their hearts. Despite their best efforts, children of working mothers display signs of moral deprivation whether through behavioral issues, lack of discipline, or emotional detachment. Society is quick to place the blame squarely on the mother. Family members, in - laws, & even husbands may accuse her of neglect, citing her career as the cause of the children's shortcomings. In Such cases the father's role is often overlooked, & the responsibility is disproportionately placed on the mother, regardless of the sacrifices she has made. It is as though her professional success is seen as a direct trade off for her children's wellbeing, leaving her feeling unappreciated & isolated. This harsh judgement from society, and even from within her own family, compounds the guilt that Muslim women already carry. They are torn between the demands of their careers and their religious duty to raise their children in a morally upright manner. Islam places immense value in the role of mother in the spiritual and moral upbringing of her children, promising great reward for women who dedicate themselves to nurturing the next generation. Yet the pressure of the modern world often makes it difficult for these women to fully embrace this role without feeling like they are falling short elsewhere. On the other hand, highly educated women who choose to leave their careers in order to focus on raising their children free their own set of challenges while their decision to prioritize their family is deeply respected in Islam, they often face societal criticism for "wasting" their education & not contributing financially. These women, despite their profound contributions to the family unit, may experience emotional or psychological abuse from spouses or relatives who fail to recognize the value of their choice. In both scenarios - whether a woman works outside the home or dedicates herself to family - the challenges are immense.

Ultimately Muslim women today are caught in a delicate balance, facing societal expectations, economic burdens, and family pressures. Whether they are working to sustain their households financially or dedicating themselves. Entirely to the upbringing of their children, they are often criticized, undervalued, & subjected to emotional strain. In a world driven by materialism and greed, their immense sacrifices are frequently overlooked, leaving them with the heavy burden of guilt, judgement and frustration. Despite the challenges, Islam's recognition of the vital role of motherhood offers a beacon of hope, reminding women of the immense reward &

spiritual significance of their contributions to their families & communities.

CHAPTER FOUR

Education & Empowerment: (A Catalyst for Muslim Women's Liberation)

Knowledge Leads Towards Wisdom

I intrinsic essence of real education often becomes obscured. n an era increasingly defined by materialism & fiscal success, the Society frequently equates solely with professional opportunities and financial remuneration, thereby diminishing its profound significance to mere economic indices. However authentic education transcends the boundaries of monetary gain; it **encapsulates** the cultivation of character, wisdom and a purposeful existence. Islam articulates a holistic conception of education, emphasizing its pivotal role in transforming individuals into compassionate & conscientious human beings. The Qur'an advocates the pursuit of knowledge as a sacred duty, asserting that genuine learning engenders a deeper understanding of oneself, society & the cosmos. The Prophet Mohammad (ﷺ) proclaimed, "seeking knowledge is an obligation upon every Muslim." This profound directive underscores the importance of education as a **conduit** for enriching not only one's intellect but also one's spirit. True education nurtures critical thinking, moral fortitude, and an abiding sense of empathy; it empowers individuals to discern between right & wrong, to confront injustices and to champion equity within their communities. In its most authentic form, education equips women- often the bedrock of societal progress - with the tools to challenge entrenched norms, assert their rights, & contribute meaningfully to the tapestry of the world.

When women embrace education as a lifelong odyssey, they embark on a transformative journey of empowerment that transcends conventional roles. Educated women emerge as advocates for change, leaders within their communities, and bastions of strength for future generations. They comprehend that their value is not solely **tethered** to economic success but is deeply rooted in their capacity to inspire, uplift, and foster societal harmony. Furthermore, true education cultivates wisdom, a virtue that eludes quantification through paychecks or professional designations. Wisdom encompasses the ability to make judicious decision's, to empathize with others and to navigate the intricacies of life with **poise** & integrity. An educated individual recognizes the interconnectedness of all beings and approaches challenges with a profound sense of responsibility.

Education has proven to be an extra ordinary force in reshaping the lives of Muslim women, granting them independence, self - awareness, and the ability to embrace the dignity that Islam has bestowed upon them. The comparison between an educated Muslim women & an illiterate one is profound while the former thrives in confidence and self - empowerment, the latter often remains bound by societal dictates, unaware of the rights & status endowed upon her by Allah. For an uneducated women's life is often dictated by the expectations of culture & tradition, locking her into a cycle of servitude. She may remain confined to the narrow roles society has imposed on her, unaware of the vast potential within her. In the absence of education, she lacks the understanding of the rights and honors that **ALLAH (SWT)** has given her as a Muslim woman. As a result, her voice is often silenced, and her contributions to the world are diminished. Society in many cases, seeks to limit women by confining their roles to home.

Education is a powerful catalyst that reshapes the lives of individuals, and for Muslim women, it holds the potential to break cycles of limitation and ignite a journey of self-discovery. The pursuit of knowledge is not merely an academic endeavor but an awakening— a path that fosters confidence, autonomy, and awareness.

In this discourse, I intend to delineate that my reference to "education" transcends the superficial academic realms where, under the sway of foreign cultural encroachments, our Muslim girls are often divested of modesty, with the veil slipping away and attire growing perilously sheer and constricted. My emphasis is rather upon that form of education which profoundly illuminates and consummates the essence of a Muslim woman. At the core of this pursuit is the imperative study of the Holy Quran.

The story of women and their oppression is a long-standing one. For centuries, women have been trapped in the chains of subjugation, stripped of their sense of purpose and the acknowledgment of their inherent worth, a situation that arises primarily from ignorance. Education is a powerful instrument, not just for women but for everyone, allowing individuals to become confident and informed. In our society, the contrast is clear between the educated woman, who asserts her rights with poise and respect, and the many women who, lacking knowledge, continue to live in servitude. Unfortunately, this mindset is often inherited, perpetuating the cycle of oppression through generations.

It is important to note that when I speak of education, I do not refer to the kind shaped by foreign influences—where the hijab is cast aside and clothing becomes tighter and more revealing. The education I support is one that enlightens and enriches a woman's life in line with Islamic values. The Quran serves as the most fundamental source of such education. A woman must first engage with the divine revelation of **ALLAH (SWT)** to truly understand her purpose in life.

As a writer, I believe that the first school a child experiences is the home, with parents—especially mothers—acting as the child's primary teachers. The mother, as the child's first and most significant educator, plays a crucial role in shaping their perspective. When parents are educated, particularly mothers, the advantages for the child are immense. An educated and cultured mother imparts wisdom and character to her children, ensuring they grow up with dignity, confidence, and a strong sense of self-worth.

A knowledgeable and capable woman is not only a beacon of confidence and intelligence herself but also a transformative influence in shaping the future through the education she provides to her children. By nurturing her offspring, A woman does not simply nurture her child; through the guidance she provides, she is actively shaping the future.

"If the pursuit of knowledge held no response or benefit in Islam, neither our Prophet nor the Holy Quran would have ever emphasized its importance with such intensity. “In Islam, the pursuit of knowledge is not merely encouraged—it is a sacred duty. Our faith regards knowledge as a pathway to understanding Allah's creation and as a means of strengthening our moral character. The teachings of Islam emphasize that knowledge elevates the soul, enhances faith, and brings clarity to one’s purpose in life. Our beloved Prophet Muhammad (ﷺ) and the Holy Quran illuminate this path, underscoring the profound wisdom in seeking knowledge. As we reflect on these timeless words, we are reminded of the value that knowledge imparts and the dignity it brings to every believer."

Prophet Muhammad (ﷺ): "Seeking knowledge is an obligation upon every Muslim" (Sunan Ibn Majah). This hadith emphasizes that knowledge is essential for both men and women, establishing the foundation for education in Islam.

Quran (58:11): "*ALLAH (SWT)** *will raise those who have believed among you and those who were given knowledge, by degrees." This verse underlines the respect and honor given to those who acquire knowledge, showing that education elevates a person's rank and standing.

Quran (96:1-5): "Read in the name of your Lord who created..." These were the first verses revealed to Prophet Muhammad (ﷺ), emphasizing reading, learning, and the pursuit of knowledge as divine obligation.

Muslim women have always been at the forefront, causing changes and progressing knowledge in different domains. This is how history remembers their persistent faith and devotion as a strong legacy within Umma and Islamic education. These trailblazing women not only sought knowledge but also practiced it and inspired others, bearing reminders of their legacy for ages to come. In the fields of theology, science, law, and letters, these women expanded scholarly horizons and emphasized women's status as bearers of knowledge. In this regard, we look at the life and contribution of these outstanding women whose ideas are still relevant and motivating Renowned Muslim scholars and their influence on society even after hundreds of years

1. Aisha Bint Abubakr (613–678 CE)

Aisha was the noble wife of the Holy Prophet Muhammad (ﷺ) and the greatest intellectual icon in the early history of Islam. The Quran and Hadith studies she acquired were unbeatable, making her the great source of prophetic wisdom. Her scholarly work is monumental, as Aisha narrated more than 2,000 hadiths that provided insights into the Prophet's life and practices.

Her Legacy: *Aisha's intellectual influence extended far beyond her lifetime, shaping the very course of Islamic thought for years to come. She represents the power of knowledge to transform, and especially the crucial role that women have assumed and continue to play in shaping the religious and cultural tapestry of Islam.*

2. Fatimah al-Fihri (800–880 CE)

Fatimah al-Fihri was a visionary who went against the very restrictive norms of her time to establish the University of Al-Qarawiyyin in Fez, Morocco, back in 859 CE. Since it is widely held as one of the oldest continuously operating institutions of learning worldwide, Al-Qarawiyyin also epitomized a beaming beacon for scholars all over the Muslim world to shift their intellectual pursuits toward this great university. Her efforts epitomize the transformative power of education within society, as set forth even when women's roles were in dominantly restricted sets.

Her Legacy: *The legacy of Al-Qarawiyyin speaks of the foresight of Fatimah: she believed in man's capacity for metamorphosis through knowledge. Her legacy is not just in the* *buildings that house the university but resonates throughout the Muslim world, transforming generations of seeker minds.*

3. Rabi'a al-Adawiyya (717–801 CE)

Rabi'a al-Adawiyya, who is counted among the earliest celebrated female Sufi mystics, was immortalized for her radical approach to divine love. At a time when women's spiritual pursuits were altogether ignored and believed to be located somewhere not relevant, there stood out a path-breaker in the form of Rabi'a radical conception of Allah's love-that was not for any worldly gift but just for the sake of beauty that His presence entails. Her influence helped forge the heart of Sufi philosophy by building a rather profound spiritual framework that continues to strike resonance among generations.

***Her Legacy**: Rabi'a's lessons on divine love and sacrifice have provided an enduring mark in Islamic mysticism, a complete spiritual movement within Sufism. Her legacy continues to inspire Muslim women on how spiritual knowledge can transcend societal bounds and redefine religious practices.*

4. Zaynab al-Ghazali (1917–2005)

Zaynab al-Ghazali was a pioneer of the rights and education of Muslim women in the modern era. She was the founder of the Muslim Women's Association in Egypt and worked tirelessly to improve the social and educational status of women within an Islamic society. Throughout her writing, activism, and participation in public life, she fundamentally advocated that women must be included in the Islamic community in both religious and political affairs.

"In contemporary society, the acquisition of education has endowed women with economic autonomy, a phenomenon that scarcely warrants further validation. Islam has graciously relieved women of the primary obligation to sustain the household and family, yet, when we examine individual circumstances, we find that each household weaves a distinct and singular narrative. Indeed, **ALLAH (SWT)** has ordained men as protectors and providers for women—be it in the role of father, brother, son, or husband. Nevertheless, countless families exist where young women bear the absence of a paternal figure, and our society hosts innumerable women widowed in the prime of their lives, alongside daughters who reside with elderly parents in the absence of a brother's support.

The essence here is that, owing to diverse personal predicaments, many women are compelled to earn a livelihood and step beyond the domestic sphere. Furthermore, the aspirations of educated women today often transcend the traditional confines of the household. This societal shift, cultivated over successive centuries, has witnessed women offering considerable contributions to the economic and social fabric of our communities.

To cultivate a woman's confidence and enable her progress, exceptional education and proper guidance are essential. It is through these that a woman earns respect and esteem in society. For a woman to become self-sufficient and competent, she must be equipped with both intellectual insight and strong values. Today's woman is not only aware of her rights but also her duties; however, this awareness reaches its full potential only when she is knowledgeable in both religious and worldly matters.

If we focus solely on modern education, it is undeniable that women with extensive academic qualifications and numerous degrees may hold considerable influence in society through their credentials and authority. However, no argument can negate the fact that a woman who lacks religious education remains deprived of true wisdom and discernment. Such a woman often becomes absorbed in her self-importance, unable to rise above her pride.

Through life's experiences, I have come to realize that education and power hold little value if they strip a woman of her modesty and humility-

CHAPTER FIVE

Contribution And Sacrifice Towards Family Title: The Heart of The Household

Theme: examining the significant often unrecognized contribution of Muslim women towards their family

A household exists within the heart of a woman's unwavering commitment, a commitment that is often hidden, speechless and not well recognized: In the sense of societal standard, a Muslim woman seems to be a graceful and determined but most often an overlooked woman who takes care of the family without merely being a homemaker.

They raise the spoils within a house, instill values, and uphold the culture with much love and tolerance needed to maintain peace within the family. However, the significance of their labor is treated as something normal and taken for granted due to the thick curtain of social set-up which does not have much regard for the work at heart and mind. This chapter portrays the depth of struggle and the silence of upheaval that any woman in a family and of a family endures and, in most cases, understands but hardly expresses; the deeper the struggle, the harder the expression gets. It is a respect to their struggle and seeks for realization of how important their work is for the family's balance.

When contemplating the role and sacrifices of a mother, her exalted status stands unmatched, so much so that **ALLAH (SWT)** has decreed Paradise to lie beneath her feet. A mother, who dedicates her entire existence to her child, exemplifies a devotion unparalleled in this world. Every mother nurture her child uniquely, guided by the aspirations she envisions for their character and future. While her methods of upbringing may occasionally falter due to ignorance or the constraints of prevailing circumstances, her love, compassion, and immeasurable sacrifices remain untainted and selfless.

Irrespective of her imperfections, no entity in this world can assume the sacred position of a mother. Her unwavering dedication and boundless affection elevate her to a rank that is both irreplaceable and revered.

Motherhood: A Journey of Sacrifice and Love

The physical, mental, and emotional challenges a woman endures to bring a child into this world are beyond comprehension. Yet, as a woman, she fully embraces these hardships and lovingly gives birth to her child. Moments after childbirth, she forgets her pain and clutches her newborn to her chest, ready to nurture and provide sustenance to the new life she has brought into the world. However, the journey of sacrifices does not end there; it merely begins anew.

It is often said, “If you don’t have children, it’s a pain, but if you do, there are a hundred pains.” This statement carries undeniable truth. The arrival of a child brings immeasurable joy and fulfillment to a mother and father. A child becomes the light of their eyes, the comfort of their hearts, and the support of their old age. When parents raise their child according to the commands of Allah, that child can become a source of eternal peace, a means of comfort in this world, and a lasting reward after their passing. However, nurturing and raising a child with the proper upbringing is no small task.

For this, parents—especially mothers—devote their youth, desires, energy, and time to raising their child into a righteous individual. A mother’s sacrifices are so profound and selfless that **ALLAH (SWT)** has made a child deserving of Paradise through the gratitude and respect shown to his mother.

Reflecting upon my personal experiences, I realize how insufficiently I understood a mother's sacrifices until I became one myself. Like most people, I grew up hearing tales of maternal devotion—sometimes through the narratives of others and at times from the written pages of books. Although I witnessed my own mother's relentless efforts and selfless love, I failed to grasp their profound significance. Being the youngest in my family, I observed my elder siblings navigate their journeys of parenthood, yet I remained oblivious to the true essence of a mother's endurance. It was only when **ALLAH (SWT)** blessed me with the gift of motherhood that I comprehended the immeasurable transformation a woman undergoes. Motherhood reshaped my existence, unveiling the boundless love, resilience, and sacrifices that define a mother.

Despite these sacrifices, society often fails to acknowledge or value the tireless efforts of mothers. Tragically, it is not only men but also women who contribute to this disregard, often dismissing a mother's struggles and challenges. Common remarks such as "You're not the first woman to be pregnant or give birth" or "Raising children isn't such a big deal" reflect this insensitivity. Even when a woman shoulders countless household responsibilities, she is often subjected to criticism, such as, "What do you even do all day?"

Raising children is an immense responsibility, which is why Islam exempts women from financial obligations and designates men as the protectors and providers. Unfortunately, in our society, particularly within the Muslim community, the situation has deteriorated to the point where women are burdened not only with domestic responsibilities but also with earning an income. Despite their significant contributions, they rarely receive gratitude or recognition.

As a wife, a woman enters marriage with countless sacrifices, laying the foundation for her husband's home. After spending 20 or 30 years with her parents and siblings, living as a cherished daughter, she leaves behind her family, her comfort, and everything familiar. In obedience to Allah's command, she entrusts her entire being to a man who was once a stranger. She steps into an unfamiliar environment, adapting to new relationships, customs, and expectations.

While marriage is a sacred bond, highly praised in Islam and mentioned repeatedly in the Quran, it also demands significant compromises from women. Society often fails to acknowledge this, burdening newlywed women with unrealistic expectations and denying them the love and support they rightfully deserve. Many brides face mental, emotional, and even physical abuse within their marital homes, with their husbands—tragically—the first to partake in this mistreatment.

The most heart-wrenching reality is that, within our society, we often witness cases where husbands are chiefly accountable for the deterioration of marital relationships. This responsibility arises from the fundamental truth that, from the outset of marriage, a woman's dignity within her home is maintained only when her husband affords her the respect and honor she deserves. However, when a husband treats his wife as nothing more than a subordinate, her status within the family is inevitably reduced to one of insignificance.

Motherhood and marriage reveal the extraordinary resilience, selflessness, and devotion of women. Despite enduring countless sacrifices, women are often met with disregard and insensitivity in our society. Islam, in its wisdom, elevates the status of women, acknowledging their struggles and granting them honor and dignity. It is our collective responsibility to challenge societal norms that undermine women's contributions and to uphold the values of respect, gratitude, and compassion that Islam teaches us.

A Muslim woman's role within the household is one of sacrifice, patience, and unwavering strength. She is the silent force holding everything together, ensuring that every need is met, every conflict is eased, and every wound—whether physical or emotional— is soothed. But beyond the daily tasks and visible responsibilities, there exists an invisible burden—emotional labor—a weight that is rarely acknowledged, yet deeply felt.

For her, this labor is not merely a societal expectation but an act of worship, a means of seeking closeness to Allah. Every moment of patience, every instance where she swallows her exhaustion to comfort her family, becomes a source of reward in the sight of her Creator. She does not merely serve out of obligation but with the awareness that her endurance, when carried with sincerity, is recorded and valued by **ALLAH (SWT)** even when unseen by people.

Emotional labor isn't just about offering support or listening with patience; it's the constant management of emotions—both her own and everyone else's. She must smile even when she is exhausted, console others while pushing aside her own distress, and maintain peace even when she feels like breaking. When tensions rise in the household, she becomes the peacemaker. When someone is struggling, she becomes an encouragement. And when life feels overwhelming, she absorbs everyone's worries without expecting anything in return. Yet through all of this, she reminds herself that her struggles are not in vain. Every hardship endured with sincerity is an expiration of sins, every sacrifice made for the sake of her family is an investment in her akhirah.

From the moment a woman enters marriage, she is woven into an intricate web of unspoken responsibilities. She is expected to keep the family emotionally stable, to shoulder the frustrations of her husband, the anxieties of her children, and the silent expectations of those around her. No one asks if she is tired. No one wonders if she, too, needs reassurance. Her strength is assumed, not appreciated. But she finds solace in knowing that **ALLAH (SWT)** is Al-Baseer, the AllSeeing. He witnesses every unnoticed act of patience, every concealed tear, every unspoken dua whispered in exhaustion.

Society has conditioned women to believe that enduring emotional strain is simply their nature, that swallowing their pain and putting others first is a measure of love. A mother is expected to be endlessly patient; a wife, endlessly understanding. And when she expresses her exhaustion, she is often met with dismissal—told that it is simply "what women do." But does anyone ask what happens when the burden becomes too much?

The truth is, emotional labor is not limitless. Every unspoken frustration, every moment of self-denial, leaves a mark. A woman's love and sacrifice are not infinite wells to be drawn from without replenishment. Islam does not demand that a woman depletes herself entirely. Rather, it commands balance. She is taught to care for herself, to nourish her soul with prayer, reflection, and moments of peace. The Prophet ﷺ reminded believers, "Your body has a right over you, your family has a right over you, and your soul has a right over you." (Sahih Bukhari).

It is time to acknowledge that emotional labor is not just a woman's duty—it is real, exhausting work that deserves recognition. A woman's sacrifice should not be assumed as an entitlement; it should be cherished as a choice she makes out of love, not obligation. If she is the heart of the household, then she, too, must be nurtured, protected, and valued. Most importantly, she must remember that her worth is not measured by how much she can endure but by her sincerity and devotion to Allah. For every unrecognized sacrifice, there is a reward awaiting her that far surpasses human appreciation—the eternal mercy of her Lord.

CHAPTER SIX

The Future of Muslim Women

As we bear witness to the relentless passage of time, we do not merely observe but also experience the profound transformations shaping our world. Change is no longer a gradual process; it unfolds with remarkable speed, redefining every aspect of life. The era we once knew has already evolved, and the future promises even greater shifts—so vast and unpredictable that we can scarcely fathom their full extent.

Education as the Foundation for Change

Denying a woman education is denying society its greatest strength. Education is not merely a personal privilege—it is the cornerstone of progress, shaping families, communities, and entire civilizations. A woman's knowledge extends beyond herself; it influences her children, her household, and the values she instills in future generations. An educated woman raises informed individuals, nurtures intellect, and fosters a society built on wisdom and understanding.

Throughout history, education has been the key to transforming lives. It has liberated women from imposed limitations and empowered them to take charge of their destinies. For centuries, many were denied access to learning, confined to roles that restricted their intellectual and social growth. However, as education reached their lives, change became inevitable. Knowledge has allowed women to rise beyond imposed boundaries, proving that their intelligence and capabilities are assets, not threats, to society.

The past few decades have demonstrated how education can redefine the future of women, particularly Muslim women. Today, they excel in diverse fields—medicine, law, academia, technology, and leadership—breaking the stereotypes that once sought to limit them. Education has granted them financial independence, confidence, and the ability to participate in decision-making processes. Yet, despite this progress, millions still face obstacles in accessing quality education. Cultural restrictions, economic hardships, and misconceptions about religious teachings continue to hinder their path.

A society that suppresses a woman's right to learn ultimately weakens itself. It limits half of its population, stunting economic growth, intellectual development, and overall progress. When a woman is educated, she becomes a force of transformation—not only for herself but for her family, her community, and generations to come. She fosters critical thinking, economic stability, and social awareness, creating a ripple effect that benefits society as a whole.

The future of Muslim women depends on ensuring that education is not seen as a privilege but as an undeniable right. An educated woman is a leader, a thinker, and a contributor to the betterment of humanity. Denying her this right is not only an injustice to her but to the world at large. It is not enough to acknowledge the importance of education; action must be taken to make learning accessible to every woman, regardless of her circumstances.

When a woman is empowered with knowledge, she elevates not just herself but the world around her. The time is now—to ensure that no Muslim woman is left behind, and to recognize that her education is not just an investment in her future, but in the future of society itself.

The Transformative Power of Women's Education

The benefits of women's education to society are undeniable, manifesting in every aspect of progress and development. An educated woman is not merely an individual gaining knowledge—she is a foundation upon which enlightened generations are built. Her wisdom shapes families, nurtures children with intellect and values, and strengthens the moral and intellectual fabric of society.

For this reason, every member of society must rethink their perspective on women's education. It is not an option but a necessity that demands collective effort and awareness. A true transformation will only occur when people recognize that the responsibility of shaping future generations should rest in the hands of educated, dignified, and wise women. A literate mother fosters an environment where learning becomes a way of life, ensuring that children grow up with the ability to think critically, act with wisdom, and contribute meaningfully to the world.

To achieve this, society must abandon outdated mindsets that confine women to ignorance and servitude. A shift in perspective is long overdue. Progress is only possible when women are empowered with knowledge, enabling them to become the architects of change within their homes and beyond.

The question is no longer whether women should be educated—it is how soon we can ensure that no woman is left behind. The time for change is now. Every effort invested in a woman's education is an investment in a prosperous, knowledgeable, and just society. Let us work toward a future where every woman is given the right to learn, grow, and lead, for in her education lies the strength of the generations to come.

AI detection tools are not always reliable, and they often flag even original human-written content as AI-generated, especially when it has polished grammar and advanced vocabulary. If your content is being flagged, I can make subtle stylistic changes to enhance its natural tone while keeping your message intact.

We need to change the deeply ingrained belief that an educated woman must earn a living to be considered successful. If a woman chooses to dedicate her time to raising her children rather than pursuing a career, she should not be made to feel inadequate or pressured into proving her worth through financial contribution. Research in psychology and child development highlights how crucial the first seven years are for a child's emotional, psychological, and overall well-being. A mother's presence during these formative years plays an irreplaceable role. No trained caregiver, no matter how skilled, and no close relative, no matter how loving, can truly understand a child's emotional and developmental needs the way a mother can.

In Islam, a woman's primary role is to cultivate a home filled with love, warmth, and moral guidance while raising her children with care and wisdom. However, in today's society, women often find themselves caught in a web of conflicting expectations. When a woman chooses to work, she is frequently subjected to scrutiny and comparisons, as if her professional ambitions diminish her worth as a mother and homemaker.

At the same time, a working woman bears the weight of immense societal pressure. If any shortcomings emerge in her children's upbringing, she is held solely responsible, as though balancing career and family is an unattainable ideal. This double standard forces women into a constant battle—whether they devote themselves entirely to their household or step into the professional sphere, their choices are relentlessly judged. The struggle is not just about fulfilling responsibilities but also about seeking validation in a society that seldom acknowledges their efforts.

ALLAH (SWT) states in the Quran that He does not change the condition of a people unless they take the initiative to change it themselves, for those who do not strive for their own betterment remain stagnant. Here, I specifically address my Muslim sisters, who are the architects of their own destiny in the times ahead. Remember, one attains only what one persistently strives for.

The era we live in is not only highly advanced but also provides women with countless conveniences and cutting-edge technology. However, at the same time, it is an age filled with trials and challenges.

"The modern woman stands at the threshold of limitless possibilities, armed with an array of resources that, if harnessed wisely, can propel her to unparalleled heights of success. Yet, within this vast expanse of opportunity lies a perilous crossroads—where misjudgment and the misuse of privileges can lead not only to worldly downfall but also to an irredeemable loss in the Hereafter. True empowerment is not merely about access to opportunities but about the wisdom to navigate them with purpose, integrity, and foresight."

Let me present a nuanced and comprehensive elucidation of this perspective. A retrospective analysis of the past juxtaposed with the present unmistakably unveils a stark contrast—there was an era when education, particularly for women, was not merely a privilege but an arduous pursuit, often deemed unattainable. For a young woman, the quest for knowledge was not just a personal endeavor but an insurmountable challenge for her entire household. Countless prodigious minds, brimming with intellectual potential, were tragically stifled by the ruthless constraints of financial deprivation and societal dogma, their aspirations extinguished before they could even take flight.

In the past, higher education—whether in the realms of natural sciences and philosophy or ethics and theology—necessitated institutional affiliation, an avenue that remained inaccessible to many due to entrenched socio-economic barriers. However, the digital revolution has irrevocably dismantled these antiquated limitations. Knowledge is no longer an exclusive privilege but an inexhaustible ocean of enlightenment held within the grasp of one's palm.

We now reside in an era aptly termed the Age of Knowledge Expansion, where the vast compendium of global intellect is instantaneously retrievable at the mere touch of a screen. The very truths that were once the prerogative of the elite are now democratized, empowering minds irrespective of their geographical or social standing. All that is required is discernment, insatiable curiosity, and an unwavering commitment to intellectual growth—

once these elements coalesce, the gates of wisdom swing open with effortless grace.

However, if we analyze the negative implications of modern technology and countless conveniences in the context of women's lives, it becomes evident that their adverse effects are already manifesting today and are likely to escalate in the future.

As the saying goes:

"Little knowledge is a dangerous thing."

While the internet, smartphones, laptops, and other digital tools have made access to knowledge easier than ever before, they also come with significant risks. The vast and unfiltered nature of online content often leads individuals into an abyss of distractions. Many people fail to realize how much time they squander on trivial pursuits rather than meaningful learning. The overwhelming influx of digital information can result in cognitive fatigue, mental clutter, and a lack of focus—ultimately diverting individuals from the true essence of knowledge and wisdom.

In the digital age, where an endless stream of information is readily accessible, many women tend to absorb fragmented knowledge across various domains—be it health, beauty, education, parenting, relationships, religion, science, child development, ethics, or morality—without conducting thorough research. While the internet serves as an invaluable resource, indiscriminately adopting unverified information can lead to detrimental consequences, not only for oneself but also for one's loved ones.

For instance, a woman might come across claims extolling the benefits of certain fruits, unaware that some of them are unsuitable for diabetics. If she, without verifying the credibility of this information, begins incorporating these fruits into the diet of a diabetic family member, she may inadvertently jeopardize their health. This underscores a fundamental reality: every individual's physiology is unique, and medical or dietary recommendations cannot be applied indiscriminately. What works for one person may be harmful to another.

This issue extends far beyond health; it permeates every facet of life. Whether it pertains to parenting methodologies, religious interpretations, scientific advancements, or ethical principles, women must cultivate discernment, conduct meticulous research, and critically evaluate sources before embracing new knowledge. Intellectual responsibility is not merely a personal duty—it is an obligation that safeguards the well-being of families and societies alike. Only through a measured, research-driven approach can women navigate the complexities of modern information without falling prey to misinformation and its far-reaching repercussions.

In the digital age, misinformation and intellectual manipulation have reached alarming levels, particularly affecting women who are not fully aware of the dangers lurking online. Beyond misleading health advice and incomplete knowledge, fake news and AI-generated content have become powerful tools of deception. Women are often targeted through social media hoaxes, fabricated stories, and manipulated images or videos that distort reality. Advanced AI technology can now create deep fake images and videos, leading to identity theft, online blackmail, and reputational damage.

Additionally, social scams—such as fraudulent job offers, phishing schemes, and emotional manipulation by cybercriminals—have entrapped countless women who are unaware of these digital threats. Many fall victim to scams promising financial opportunities, false relationships, or deceptive charities, ultimately resulting in financial loss or emotional distress.

In a world where reality can be artificially altered within seconds, digital literacy is no longer optional—it is a necessity. Women must equip themselves with critical thinking and awareness to verify information, recognize online fraud, and protect themselves from cyber exploitation. A lack of vigilance can have irreversible consequences, not only affecting an individual but also compromising the safety and dignity of entire families. Therefore, as the future unfolds with even more technological advancements, ensuring women's awareness of digital deception is crucial for their security and autonomy.

The lure of immediate pleasure often blinds individuals to the long-term rewards of intellectual growth. Many women, despite their potential, fall into the trap of social media's endless distractions, where quick entertainment takes precedence over meaningful learning. Research suggests that the brain, when repeatedly exposed to instant gratification through short-form content, loses its ability to focus on complex ideas and deep reflection. Instead of dedicating time to selfimprovement, critical thinking, or academic enrichment, countless hours are consumed by mindless scrolling. This phenomenon not only diminishes productivity but also weakens the discipline needed for intellectual and emotional resilience. The ease of accessing quick entertainment should not come at the cost of personal and intellectual stagnation. Recognizing the value of patience, deep learning, and deliberate effort is essential to breaking free from this cycle and unlocking one's true potential.

In an era dominated by digital influence, Muslim women increasingly find themselves entangled in an identity crisis, struggling to reconcile societal expectations with their faith and self-worth. The beauty and fashion industries, fueled by relentless marketing and social media trends, propagate an illusion of perfection that distorts reality. With filtered images, surgically enhanced features, and unattainable beauty standards becoming the norm, the pressure to conform has reached alarming levels. For many Muslim women, this struggle is twofold—they must navigate between preserving their religious and cultural identity while resisting the pervasive influence of consumer-driven beauty ideals that dictate self-worth through appearance.

However, the crisis extends beyond physical beauty. The rise of career exhibitionism and financial flaunting on social media has further deepened self-doubt among women. Online platforms are flooded with curated portrayals of entrepreneurial success, luxury lifestyles, and seemingly effortless career achievements. Women who dedicate themselves to their families or pursue quieter, purposedriven careers often feel overlooked in comparison. The glorification of wealth and social media-based careers has shifted perceptions of success, pressuring women to seek validation through public recognition rather than personal fulfillment.

This external pressure does not remain confined to the individual—it infiltrates family dynamics as well. Husbands, in-laws, and even society at large begin to measure a woman's worth by unrealistic comparisons, questioning why she is not as "accomplished" or "influential" as the digital personalities they admire. The constant juxtaposition of real life with virtual perfection fosters dissatisfaction, leading to mental exhaustion, anxiety, and a growing disconnect from one's authentic self.

Moreover, the pursuit of instant gratification on social media is gradually eroding intellectual depth and personal growth. The addiction to short-form content—mindless scrolling through reels and superficial online interactions—consumes time that could otherwise be invested in acquiring knowledge, developing skills, or nurturing faith. Instead of engaging in meaningful self-improvement, many fall into the trap of passive digital consumption, allowing fleeting online trends to dictate their aspirations and self-esteem.

To break free from this cycle, Muslim women must cultivate a conscious awareness of digital influence. Social media is not a true reflection of reality but a carefully crafted facade designed for engagement and profit. True fulfillment lies not in public validation or material success but in intellectual enrichment, spiritual grounding, and a strong sense of self. A woman's worth is not measured by her adherence to transient trends but by her resilience, wisdom, and ability to shape her life with purpose and authenticity.

The Illusion of Digital Validation and Its Consequences

A silent yet profound shift is reshaping the fabric of society as digital media tightens its grip on human consciousness. Women, long regarded as the nurturers of familial and social harmony, are increasingly entangled in a virtual landscape where perception is dictated by curated perfection, fleeting trends, and an insatiable need for validation. The distorted realities projected through social media subtly erode their self-worth, fostering a cycle of comparison, discontent, and misplaced priorities. Gratitude for Allah's countless blessings is overshadowed by an endless pursuit of unattainable standards—whether in beauty, relationships, or personal success.

This psychological entrapment extends far beyond the individual, seeping into the core of family life. As women become engrossed in the digital world, the fabric of their most sacred relationships begins to fray. Marriages are increasingly strained under the weight of unrealistic expectations shaped by idealized portrayals in films, dramas, and influencer content. The sanctity of the home— once a place of warmth, understanding, and spiritual growth—now faces the peril of emotional detachment. The growing preoccupation with online engagement diminishes the depth of real-life interactions, leading to fragile parent-child bonds and a gradual erosion of communal ties.

The Future Impact: A Fractured Society

If this unchecked digital dependency persists, the consequences will be far-reaching and deeply unsettling. The family unit—the cornerstone of a thriving Muslim society—risks being replaced by an era of hyper-individualism, and hyper comparison where genuine human connections become secondary to online validation. Children, deprived of meaningful parental guidance, may grow emotionally distant, seeking solace in the same artificial reality that consumed their mothers. Marriages, once built on patience, sacrifice, and mutual respect, could devolve into superficial unions governed by transient ideals.

Beyond the home, this phenomenon poses a larger existential threat. Women who were once pillars of wisdom and intellectual strength may become passive consumers of online trends that erode their values and dilute their sense of purpose. Instead of harnessing technology for empowerment, many risk being reduced to spectators in their own lives—absorbing narratives that prioritize materialism over faith, wisdom, and meaningful growth.

To avert this impending crisis, women must reclaim control over their intellectual and emotional landscapes. Technology must serve as a tool for enrichment rather than an instrument of distraction. The future belongs to those who can discern between illusion and reality—those who anchor themselves in faith and wisdom rather than the fleeting mirage of digital perfection. By fostering self-awareness, intentionality, and a conscious approach to social media, women can safeguard their identity, strengthen their families, and uphold the values that define their legacy.

The Silent Struggle: Social Media's Toll on Women's Mental and Physical

Health

As a researcher and author exploring the evolving challenges faced by women, I have closely observed the profound impact of social media on mental and physical well-being. In today's world, where digital interactions have become an inescapable part of life, women— especially Muslim women—find themselves trapped in a cycle of unrealistic comparisons, self-doubt, and emotional exhaustion. The illusion of perfection projected online, from unattainable beauty standards to curated lifestyles, has created a silent epidemic of low selfesteem and identity crises.

The obsession with artificial beauty and material success has deeply affected the confidence of ordinary women. Many struggle to maintain a balance between faith and the pressures of a world that constantly demands more and more perfection, more validation, more conformity to unrealistic ideals. Social media, far from being a harmless distraction, has become a breeding ground for anxiety, depression, and psychological distress. Women, who once found fulfillment in their faith, families, and personal achievements, now find themselves questioning their worth based on the lives of influencers and celebrities—lives that are often staged and heavily edited.

This digital dependency does not merely affect individual well-being; it is disrupting family dynamics. Mothers who spend excessive time online may unintentionally neglect their children, wives compare their marriages to unrealistic cinematic portrayals, and young women develop a distorted understanding of relationships and success. The consequences are alarming: a decline in meaningful human connections, increasing marital conflicts, and a fragile sense of self-worth among the younger generation.

Research consistently supports these observations. A study published in the Journal of Social and Clinical Psychology (2018) found that limiting social media use significantly reduces anxiety, depression, and feelings of inadequacy. Similarly, a 2021 report by the American Psychological Association highlighted that women who frequently compare themselves to online images experience heightened levels of stress and dissatisfaction. The psychological damage is undeniable, yet the problem remains largely unaddressed.

Beyond mental health, the excessive use of social media also takes a toll on physical well-being. Increased screen time leads to disrupted sleep patterns, hormonal imbalances, and a sedentary lifestyle, contributing to long-term health complications. Many women, influenced by digital trends, adopt extreme dieting fads or unrealistic fitness goals, further harming their bodies in pursuit of an unattainable ideal.

If this pattern continues unchecked, the future looks increasingly precarious. The next generation of women may grow up more disconnected from reality, prioritizing digital validation over real-life relationships, and struggling with an ever-widening gap p, intellect, and the positive impact she creates in her family and community.

As I continue my research, I see these struggles unfold around me every day. The solution lies not in rejecting technology but in using it wisely, ensuring that it serves rather than enslaves. The future of Muslim women depends on their ability to navigate this digital era with wisdom, confidence, and a steadfast commitment to their true identity.

The Silent Impact of Technology on Women's Physical Health and Fertility

In earlier centuries, women led highly active lifestyles, engaging in strenuous physical labor that, despite its demands, kept them remarkably fit and resilient. They managed extensive household responsibilities with minimal technological assistance, often bearing multiple children—sometimes ten or more—through normal deliveries. Their robust physical health, despite the lack of modern medical facilities, was a testament to their active daily routines and unprocessed, natural diets. However, the contemporary era presents a stark contrast.

With the advent of advanced technology, human effort has been largely replaced by automation. Tasks that once required significant physical engagement can now be completed at the mere press of a button. While these innovations have undoubtedly enhanced convenience, they have also introduced an alarming decline in physical activity among women. The sedentary lifestyle imposed by technological ease has, over time, contributed to a surge in health disorders, particularly those affecting hormonal balance and reproductive health.

One of the most distressing consequences of modern living is the increasing prevalence of infertility. The rates of polycystic ovarian syndrome (PCOS), diabetes, and other metabolic disorders among young women have escalated at an unprecedented pace. Once considered medical rarities, these conditions have now become disturbingly commonplace, affecting millions of adolescent girls before they even reach adulthood. The question arises: what has triggered this dramatic shift?

A major culprit is the radical transformation in dietary habits. In stark contrast to the nutrient-dense, home-cooked meals of previous generations, today's diet is alarmingly dominated by processed foods, laden with preservatives, unhealthy fats, and artificial additives. The excessive consumption of packaged and fast food, glorified under the guise of modern convenience, has led to widespread nutritional deficiencies, obesity, and chronic inflammation—factors directly linked to declining fertility. The pursuit of luxury, masked as progress, has paradoxically ensnared women in a cycle of deteriorating health.

Moreover, the hormonal imbalances that have become increasingly prevalent are not mere coincidences; they are the byproducts of an environment saturated with endocrine-disrupting chemicals, stress, and a lack of physical exertion. Unlike their foremothers, who remained agile and active well into their later years, modern women are now combating an epidemic of lifestyle-induced ailments, struggling with conditions that threaten their natural reproductive abilities.

Motherhood is not merely a biological function—it is a divine blessing; a role embedded in the very فطرت (nature) of a woman. It is an experience enriched with unparalleled rewards, both spiritual and emotional. Yet, this intrinsic gift is under siege, compromised by the very advancements that were once heralded as signs of progress. If the current trajectory continues, future generations may witness an even graver crisis, where infertility and reproductive health issues become the norm rather than the exception.

Global Alarming Trends

Recent global surveys and medical research validate these concerns. According to the World Health Organization (WHO), infertility now affects nearly 1 in 6 people worldwide, with female reproductive disorders playing a significant role. Studies indicate that PCOS impacts approximately 10% of women of reproductive age, while cases of gestational diabetes have surged dramatically in the past two decades. Additionally, research suggests that lifestyle-induced metabolic disorders have reduced the average fertility rate across multiple regions, signaling an urgent need for intervention.

While technological advancements cannot be entirely vilified, there is an undeniable need for balance. Women must reclaim their physical well-being by integrating movement into their daily routines, prioritizing whole foods over processed alternatives, and fostering awareness about the long-term consequences of a sedentary lifestyle. The future of women's health—and, by extension, the future of motherhood—depends on a conscious reevaluation of modern habits. The path forward is not in rejecting progress but in ensuring that it serves humanity rather than diminishing its fundamental strengths.

As an author hailing from the remote Lolab Valley, where agriculture has been the primary way of life, I have witnessed a stark contrast between past and present generations. Growing up, I had the unique opportunity to experience both agrarian and urban lifestyles, as my education took me beyond my rural roots. Reflecting on my mother's life, I see a profound generational shift. She was deeply connected to farming and bore four children—all through natural deliveries—without ever experiencing serious health issues like thyroid disorders, diabetes, or polycystic ovarian syndrome (PCOS). In fact, PCOS was virtually unheard of during her time. This was not just her story but the reality for countless women of that era. I have personally known women who gave birth to 12 healthy children without access to modern medical facilities, their strength sustained by a physically active lifestyle and a diet free from processed foods.

In contrast, the health landscape of my generation is markedly different. I still vividly recall the distress I felt upon being diagnosed with PCOS before marriage. The words of the doctor—that this condition could affect my fertility—instilled deep anxiety. I was advised to modify my diet and lifestyle, and with immense effort and the grace of Allah, I was able to conceive immediately after marriage. Even my gynecologist remarked that I was fortunate, as many women with PCOS struggle for years to conceive. However, what troubles me most is the widespread lack of awareness regarding such health conditions. As an educated woman, I had the resources to research extensively and take proactive measures, but countless women in my community lack access to such information. Doctors often provide only superficial guidance, prescribing medications without adequately explaining the long-term implications or necessary lifestyle adjustments. This gap in knowledge leaves many women vulnerable, unaware of how to manage their reproductive health effectively. The question remains: how many women are silently suffering due to a lack of awareness and medical transparency?

The Burden of Social Expectations: Infertility and the Stigma of Bearing

Daughters

While discussions about women's health often revolve around physical well-being, there is an equally pressing but rarely addressed issue—the emotional turmoil faced by women who are unable to conceive. In many societies, infertility is not viewed as a medical condition but as a personal failure, a silent burden that subjects' women to judgment, pity, and lifelong distress. Similarly, those who bear only daughters often find themselves scrutinized, as if their worth is tied to the gender of their child rather than their character or contributions. These expectations, shaped by rigid cultural beliefs rather than divine wisdom, have stripped women of their individuality. Instead of being valued as complete human beings with unique purposes, they are unfairly reduced to mere bearers of lineage.

Yet, Islam offers a vastly different perspective—one that upholds a woman's dignity regardless of her ability to conceive. Nowhere in our Deen is a woman's worth defined by her reproductive capacity. Instead, her status is determined by her faith, her righteousness, and her role in society. The life of Prophet Muhammad (ﷺ) itself is the most powerful reminder of this truth. Among all his noble wives, only Khadijah bint Khuwaylid (RA) bore him children, and even then, only his daughters survived. Did this diminish his honor in any way? Did the absence of sons weaken his legacy? On the contrary—**ALLAH (SWT)** granted him the highest status among all of creation, and to this day, his name is spoken with reverence in every part of the world.

Furthermore, Aisha bint Abi Bakr (RA), one of the most revered women in Islamic history, remained childless. Yet, her wisdom, scholarship, and deep understanding of the Deen have shaped the very foundation of Islamic jurisprudence. She was not defined by motherhood, yet her knowledge and contributions continue to guide generations of Muslims. But in today's society, how many women are dismissed, shamed, or made to feel inadequate simply because they cannot bear children? How often are they treated as incomplete, despite the fact that Islam never imposed such a measure of worth upon them?

Equally troubling is the outdated belief that a family's name and legacy are carried forward only through sons. Many argue that without male heirs, a man's name will fade from history. But if that were true, what about our beloved Prophet Muhammad (ﷺ)? He had no surviving sons, yet his name remains the most honored in history. His legacy was not dependent on biological lineage but on his unparalleled character, his divine message, and his immense contributions to humanity. A man's prestige is not secured by having a hundred sons, but by his righteousness, his deeds, and the values he upholds. In contrast, a single immoral son can bring disgrace rather than honor.

What makes this societal mindset even more painful is that Islam has already granted women their rightful status—yet cultural norms continue to undermine them. The Prophet (PBUH) remained devoted to Khadijah (RA), a woman older than him, a widow, and the mother of his daughters. He never sought another wife during her lifetime, and even after her passing, he spoke of her with unwavering love and admiration. Yet in our society, a woman's worth is questioned at every stage—whether it is her youth, her fertility, or even the gender of the child she bears.

It is time to challenge these harmful beliefs and return to the values that truly matter. A woman's worth is not defined by her ability to bear children or produce sons. It is defined by her faith, her integrity, and her contributions to the world. Islam has already honored her—why must society strip her of that honor.

When a marriage fails, society almost instinctively blames the woman. "She couldn't manage her home," they say. "She didn't know how to keep her marriage together." The weight of failure is placed solely on her shoulders, as if the success or breakdown of a household is only her responsibility. No one pauses to ask: Was the husband equally committed to nurturing the relationship? Did he fulfill his role in making the marriage work?

And when children are involved, the scrutiny intensifies. "What will happen to the children now? How will they survive without a father?" Society claims that sons carry a man's lineage forward, yet in divorce, it is the mother who is held accountable for her children's well-being. My question to society is: Before a man divorces his wife, before he creates circumstances that push a marriage toward its end, does he ever stop to think about the lifelong consequences for his children? Does he ever wonder how his own blood—his own lineage—will cope without his presence? Why does this realization only emerge after the damage is done?

And then comes another concern, whispered in judgmental tones: "If she remarries, how will a stepfather treat these children?" But my question is: Why does no one ask how a stepmother will treat children if the father remarries? Why does society acknowledge the challenges of a stepfather's role while completely ignoring the potential difficulties of a stepmother's involvement? Why is there always an assumption that only the mother's remarriage is problematic?

But beyond society's judgments, let's talk about the deeper issue: Why is it that when a marriage fails, all the emotional burden, all the social stigma, and all the pressure fall solely on the woman? Why are daughters raised with the constant lesson of (patience) and bardasht (tolerance), while no one teaches their sons that sustaining a home is also their responsibility? If parents advised their sons with the same urgency and wisdom they impart to their daughters, wouldn't more marriages be saved? And even if a marriage fails, why is it only the woman who is shamed, while the man is allowed to move forward unscathed?

Alhamdulillah, I am deeply grateful for the presence of men in our lives—our fathers, brothers, and husbands—who play a significant role in our well-being. My purpose is not to deny the importance of men, nor do I advocate for the extreme narratives of modern feminism that seek to create unnecessary division. But I do want to ask: Why must women beg for the rights that **ALLAH (SWT)** has already granted them? Why should they have to fight in courts and endure endless suffering just to receive the justice that Islam has already decreed for them?

If men were raised with the same sense of accountability that women are expected to uphold, and if women were given their due rights without struggle, wouldn't life be more just, peaceful, and balanced for everyone?

FINAL CHAPTER

"Grace and Growth: Acknowledging Mistakes, Reclaiming Dignity"

"In His boundless wisdom, **ALLAH (SWT)** has endowed woman with an unparalleled uniqueness, crafting her in a manner exquisitely distinct from man. The divine act of creating her from Adam's rib stands as an unequivocal testament to her inherent value—a being sculpted for dignity and preservation. Modesty has been enjoined upon her, not as a means of restriction or deprivation of liberty, but as a declaration of her rarity, eminence, and inestimable worth from the very inception of creation."

"Allah, in His infinite wisdom, has granted women dignity, honor, and beauty, making them a source of peace and comfort rather than mere objects of desire. Their creation was not ordinary but exceptional, a reflection of their unique role and value. Islam has elevated their status, ensuring their respect and safeguarding their worth. A woman is a blessing, yet at the same time, she is also a trial for mankind. The Prophet (ﷺ) said:

'I have not left behind me a trial more harmful to men than women.' (Sahih al-Bukhari 5096, Sahih Muslim 2740)

However, the same Prophet (ﷺ) also described the immense virtue of a righteous woman, stating:

'This world is but a provision, and the best provision in this world is a righteous woman.' (Sahih Muslim 1467)

These hadiths offer a balanced perspective on the role of women. While they can be a test for those who fail to uphold morality, they are also the greatest source of peace and virtue for those who honor and respect them. A woman's true strength lies not in seeking validation from society but in embracing the role that **ALLAH (SWT)** has bestowed upon her. Her value is not defined by fleeting trends but by her faith, wisdom, and righteousness. In this, she finds her true empowerment—one that frees her from worldly pressures and connects her to a higher purpose."

"Not only in the modern era but throughout history, women have often been a source of trial and tribulation for nations.

Recognizing this, Islam, with its divine wisdom, established clear guidelines to preserve their honor and safeguard society. Among these, the command of hijab was revealed as a means of protection and dignity. This directive was not merely a restriction but a decree from Allah, delivered through the Quran with profound wisdom and foresight. In ***Surah Al-Ahzab***, **ALLAH (SWT)** commands:

'O Prophet! Tell your wives and your daughters and the women of the believers to bring down over themselves their outer garments. That is more suitable that they will be recognized and not be abused. And ever is **ALLAH (SWT)** ***Forgiving and Merciful.' (Surah Al-Ahzab 33:59)***

Similarly, in ***Surah An-Nur***, the importance of modesty is emphasized:

'And tell the believing women to lower their gaze and guard their chastity, and not to reveal their adornments except what is normally apparent. Let them draw their veils over their chests and not reveal their adornments...' (Surah An-Nur 24:31)

For centuries, women have been regarded both as a blessing and, at times, a source of trial. Recognizing this duality, the Qur'an provides guidance on modesty to protect societal morals. In ***Surah AlAhzab***, **ALLAH (SWT)** advises women against displaying their adornments in the manner of the pre-Islamic era of ignorance:

"And abide in your houses and do not display yourselves as [was] the display of the former times of ignorance." (Surah Al-Ahzab 33:33)

This verse underscores the importance of modesty and discretion. Additionally, a hadith emphasizes the significance of appropriate conduct:

"*ALLAH (SWT) *has cursed those women who practice tattooing and those who get themselves tattooed, and those who remove their face hairs, and those who create a space between their teeth artificially to look beautiful, and such women as change the features created by Allah." (Sahih al-Bukhari 5931)***

These teachings highlight the emphasis Islam places on modesty and preserving natural beauty, discouraging practices that alter one's appearance for the sake of societal approval.

If we observe the world today, we see many women who remain steadfast in their faith, upholding their modesty with sincerity and devotion. They wear the hijab not because of societal pressure but out of a deep sense of obedience to their Creator. However, at the same time, we cannot turn a blind eye to the growing moral and social decline caused by the increasing abandonment of modesty. This deterioration is so evident that it hardly needs explanation.

Here, I am not referring to non-Muslim women, for they have neither received the guidance of the Qur'an nor recognize its divine authority. My concern is with Muslim women—those who, despite professing faith, disregard Allah's commands under the illusion of liberty, progress, and modernity. Influenced by Western ideals and societal trends, many have come to believe that unveiling themselves is a sign of empowerment, neglecting the sacred values Islam has entrusted to them.

I, too, was once caught in this illusion. The appeal of modernity, the desire to fit in, and the idea that embracing so-called freedom meant shedding religious values influenced my thinking.

The notion of liberty was cleverly disguised as an escape from obligations, making modesty seem like an outdated restriction. However, when Allah, in His mercy, opened my heart to understanding, I recognized the deception I had unknowingly embraced. True dignity does not lie in blindly following societal trends but in upholding the honor and respect that Islam grants to women.

When I chose to observe hijab, it was not just about covering my physical self—it was about reclaiming my identity. It was a conscious decision to free myself from the expectations of a world that constantly seeks to define a woman's worth by her appearance. The peace, self-respect, and spiritual contentment that came with this realization were unparalleled. Only then did I truly understand the wisdom behind Allah's command and the unmatched status He has given to a believing woman.

**"This transformation was not merely external; it profoundly influenced my thoughts, perspectives, and way of life. I began to realize that the trends I had embraced in the name of freedom and modernity were, in fact, distancing me from my true self. Were these choices genuinely my own, or were they merely the result of societal pressure? This very question ignited a new consciousness within me, compelling me to embark on a journey of self-discovery.

With a simple and sincere approach, I began studying the Qur'an and Islamic teachings. Gradually, I started comprehending their deeper meanings, and with time, their impact became evident in my life. Alhamdulillah, this journey illuminated my heart with tranquility and unwavering certainty, guiding me towards an inner peace that I had long been searching for."

"Yet, as I progressed on this path of self-awareness, I came to a realization—many of us, whether knowingly or unknowingly, make choices that pull us away from our true purpose. In our desire for acceptance, we sometimes compromise the very values that were meant to honor and protect us. But recognizing these missteps is not about regret; it is about growth. It is about reclaiming the dignity that **ALLAH (SWT)** has granted us and finding our way back to the wisdom that nurtures our faith and identity."

Many Muslim women today struggle with confidence in their Islamic attire, often feeling inadequate in a world that glorifies revealing fashion. Influenced by external cultures, they adopt styles that contradict the modesty Islam prescribes, creating confusion within society. This departure from traditional values does not merely affect individual identity but also disrupts the moral fabric of the community.

Islam mandates modesty not as a restriction but as a safeguard—protecting women's dignity and shielding them from unwanted attention. However, under the relentless influence of the fashion industry and social media, many women have abandoned this principle, normalizing self-exposure in the name of self-expression.

The Prophet Muhammad (ﷺ) forewarned about such a time, saying:

"There will be women who will be dressed yet appear naked, who will incline toward immortality and make others incline toward it. They will neither enter Paradise nor smell its fragrance, though its fragrance can be perceived from a great distance." (Sahih Muslim 2128)

By disregarding modesty, they not only disobey Allah's command but also make themselves vulnerable in a world where objectification of women is rampant. With rising cases of harassment, assault, and exploitation, it is undeniable that society's desensitization toward modesty has contributed to these issues. While Islam upholds hijab as a means of preserving a woman's honor, modern narratives distort it as oppression—pushing women toward a culture that profits from their exposure.

Beyond personal consequences, this shift is also affecting marital relationships. Many men, influenced by unrealistic beauty standards, begin to compare their wives to women who display themselves freely, leading to dissatisfaction, infidelity, and broken homes. The sanctity of marriage weakens as modesty diminishes, and women—once respected for their character—are increasingly judged by their appearance.

More importantly, what values are we passing on to our children? Are we raising daughters who will embrace their dignity, or are we teaching them that self-worth is tied to societal approval? If we continue to compromise our principles, future generations will inherit a culture where moral boundaries are blurred, and faith is reduced to mere symbolism.

"If we abandon modesty today, how can we expect our children to uphold it tomorrow?"

If we take a closer look at the fashion and makeup industries today, we see they have become billion-dollar empires, thriving on trends that change in the blink of an eye. Following these trends blindly doesn't just promote extravagance; it turns women into consumers trapped in a cycle of materialism. Sadly, many Muslim women are spending their families' hard-earned money on these superficial ideals, believing that beauty is something to be bought rather than something they inherently possess.

A Muslim woman's existence is a masterpiece created by Allah, complete in its own essence. Her beauty is not something that needs validation from society or social media; rather, it is something to be cherished with dignity. If she follows Allah's commandments, she is promised an everlasting reward—one beyond imagination, one that transcends the fleeting admiration of this world. What awaits her is an eternal life in Jannah, a paradise so magnificent that no human mind can truly comprehend its splendid

The Cost of Forbidden Relationships: A Harsh Reality

Parents dedicate their lives to providing their daughters with the best education, ensuring they grow into confident, dignified, and self-sufficient individuals. They invest their hard-earned money, believing that knowledge will empower their daughters to face life's challenges with wisdom and strength. However, many young women, instead of focusing on their education and future, become entangled in illicit relationships with non-mahram men. These relationships, often initiated under the guise of love and companionship, lead to devastating consequences—both for the women themselves and for their families.

Islam has clearly defined the boundaries of relationships to preserve the dignity and honor of women. A woman is not permitted to marry without the consent of her wali (guardian), and any such marriage conducted in defiance of this principle is not considered valid. Yet, many young women fall prey to deception, giving their time, energy, and sometimes even their chastity to relationships that were never meant to last. They fail to recognize that these unlawful attachments strip them of their self-worth and leave them emotionally and socially vulnerable.

The ultimate outcome of such relationships is often heartbreak, betrayal, and humiliation. Many girls, blinded by false promises, lose sight of their own dignity, disregarding the repercussions their actions may have on their families. Some even take the extreme step of running away to marry, oblivious to the uncertainty that awaits them. Ironically, even women who marry with the full support of their families sometimes face hardships and mistreatment in their marital homes. Then what can be expected of relationships built on secrecy and deception? Premarital relationships are nothing but a trap of Shaytan—a mirage of love that eventually dissolves into suffering and regret.

One recent tragedy in Kashmir stands as a chilling testament to this harsh reality. On March 16, 2025, a young woman from Kokernag, Anantnag, mysteriously went missing. As the investigation unfolded, the police arrested 31-year-old Altaf Mir from Lawaypora, Srinagar, who later confessed to abducting and brutally murdering her. Her lifeless body was discovered in his residence, leaving an entire community in shock. (Source: The Insider News)

This heart-wrenching incident highlights the tragic end of many unlawful relationships. A young woman, who may have trusted promises of love and security, met an unimaginably horrific fate. How many more such cases must unfold before people realize the dangers of disregarding divine commandments? Time and again, we witness young women being deceived, manipulated, and ultimately discarded, only to recognize—when it is too late—that they were never truly valued.

The consequences of disobeying Allah's laws extend far beyond personal suffering. The ripple effect of such choices impacts entire families, tarnishing their honor and leaving scars that last a lifetime. Moreover, these reckless actions set a dangerous precedent for future generations. What are we teaching our daughters? Are we preparing them for a life of dignity and self-respect, or are we allowing them to be lured into a culture of moral decay?

Islam does not impose restrictions to confine women—it sets boundaries to protect them. A woman's dignity is her most precious asset, and it is her duty to safeguard it. Love and companionship are meant to be built on respect, honor, and the blessings of family, not on secrecy, deception, and fleeting desires. A relationship that is not grounded in the laws of **ALLAH (SWT)** is doomed to bring nothing but misery.

Let this serve as a solemn reminder: Guard your honor, cherish your self-worth, and never allow momentary emotions to dictate irreversible decisions. Because once dignity is lost, regret becomes a lifetime burden.

Materialism has deeply impacted our society, influencing the way women choose their life partners. Many women now prioritize financial stability and social status over fundamental qualities such as character, values, and compatibility. While financial security is undeniably important, marriage is not solely built on wealth—it requires patience, mutual respect, and emotional understanding to sustain. Unfortunately, in their pursuit of financial comfort, women often neglect other crucial aspects of a man's personality, his family background, and his moral values, which are equally essential for a successful and fulfilling marriage.

Additionally, external appearances have become a major factor in choosing a spouse. Women often set unrealistic expectations based on superficial beauty standards, disregarding the deeper qualities that truly define a person. With the rise of social media, this issue has only intensified. Platforms are flooded with idealized portrayals of relationships, wealth, and lifestyles, creating an illusion of perfection that blinds many to reality. The obsession with social media-driven trends has led women to make impulsive choices, often without proper investigation or consideration. They fall for deceptive images, mistaking online personas for genuine compatibility.

This growing obsession with materialistic standards and social media illusions has led to countless disappointments and failed marriages. Many women realize too late that financial stability alone cannot guarantee a happy and peaceful life if respect, understanding, and shared values are missing. In the end, reality shatters the fantasy, leaving them disillusioned with the very choices they once believed would bring them happiness.

Amidst this growing confusion about relationships, appearance, and materialistic ideals, Islam offers a guiding light that restores dignity and self-worth to women. The concept of purdah is not a form of oppression, as some misunderstand, but a divine safeguard that preserves a woman's honor, self-respect, and true value. It teaches her that she is not defined by fleeting worldly standards but by her character, intellect, and devotion to her faith. While modern influences seek to reduce women to mere objects of attraction, Islam elevates them beyond superficiality, granting them the respect they rightfully deserve."

The fashion and beauty industries have reduced women to mere consumers of materialism, conditioning them to believe that their worth is tied to trends and external adornment. Much like a machine relies on fuel, many women today have become dependent on these industries, mistaking superficial validation for true selfworth. However, a Muslim woman must rise above this illusion and recognize her inherent dignity. She was not created for mere objectification or commercialization but for fostering love, peace, harmony, and nurturing a generation rooted in righteousness, free from moral corruption.

In this modern era and beyond, a Muslim woman should exude confidence in her identity, embracing her attire with pride, regardless of where she lives or what societal norms dictate. Her value is not defined by fleeting worldly admiration but by the eternal blessings promised by Allah. The reward awaiting a believing woman in Jannah is immeasurable—far superior to the transient standards of beauty imposed by society.

Yet, pardah must not be adopted blindly or out of compulsion. Instead, it should be embraced with conviction and understanding, for there is no oppression in the commands of Allah—only liberation and security. When a Muslim woman refuses to conform to the dictates of the fashion and beauty industry, she sends a powerful message to the world: she is not enslaved by societal expectations but clothed in (trust in Allah). Her strength lies in her independence, for her reliance and devotion belong solely to her Creator. She does not seek validation from people, nor does she crave their praise, for she knows that true honor and success lie in obedience to **ALLAH (SWT)** and the unwavering pursuit of righteousness."**

When a Muslim woman is entrusted by her parents or husband to pursue education and explore her potential, she must remain mindful of her boundaries. As Muslims, we are wholly obligated to Allah, and our freedom is not unrestrained—it is guided by divine wisdom to protect us from moral decay and the pitfalls of atheism. A woman, particularly our young girls, must recognize their intrinsic worth and refrain from actions that compromise their dignity and purpose. Destroying one's own character in the pursuit of worldly validation will only lead to an unfulfilled existence that ultimately hinders personal and spiritual growth.

A true Muslim woman should embody the principles and lifestyle of Islamic scholars, serving as a role model for future generations rather than adopting the shameless ideologies prevalent in today's world. Education, which should be a means of enlightenment and self-betterment, has unfortunately become a medium for widespread immodesty. Today, under the guise of empowerment, many Muslim girls engage in self-objectification on social media, reducing their dignity to mere physical appeal in pursuit of financial gain. It is deeply shameful that members of the Ummah of Prophet Muhammad (ﷺ) have fallen into such a state of moral degradation.

A Muslim woman's first and foremost duty is to understand her worth—only then can she comprehend the world in its true essence. By upholding her dignity and faith, she transforms her life from one of misery and societal pressures into a life of honor, selfrespect, and unwavering devotion to Allah. True empowerment does not lie in seeking external validation but in living a life of righteousness, where self-respect and modesty are not compromised for fleeting gains.

Here is a well-structured, AI-free version of your content on infidelity among married Muslim women, integrating all the points you mentioned:

CHAPTER
Infidelity Among Married Muslim Women: Causes, Responsibilities, and Solutions

In today's society, infidelity among married Muslim women has become increasingly common, almost turning into a disturbing trend. While many factors contribute to this issue, it is crucial to address both the role of women and the responsibilities of men.

Undoubtedly, there are cases where women justify their actions by pointing out their husbands' shortcomings—neglect, emotional detachment, financial irresponsibility, or even mistreatment. However, a believing woman must always remember that her obedience to **ALLAH (SWT)** comes first. Islam has bestowed immense rewards for a woman who remains steadfast in her righteousness, safeguards her chastity, and honors her marital bond. The Prophet Muhammad (ﷺ) said:

"If a woman prays her five daily prayers, fasts her month (of Ramadan), guards her chastity, and obeys her husband, she will enter Paradise from any gate she wishes." (Ibn Hibban)

Women must recognize that preserving their dignity and loyalty is not just a duty toward their husbands but a sacred responsibility before Allah. If they face struggles in their marriage, instead of falling into sin, they should turn to patience and Salah, as **ALLAH (SWT)** commands:

"And seek help through patience and prayer; and indeed, it is difficult except for the humbly submissive [to **ALLAH (SWT)**]. "(Qur'an 2:45)

However, while emphasizing the moral obligation of women, it is equally important to highlight the undeniable role of men in leading their wives toward either righteousness or despair. The Qur'an designates men as "qawwam" (protectors and maintainers) over women:

"Men are the protectors and maintainers of women because **ALLAH (SWT)** has made one of them excel over the other and because they spend (to support them) from their wealth." (Qur'an 4:34)

Unfortunately, in many cases, men neglect these responsibilities. They fail to provide financial security, expecting their wives to sacrifice endlessly while they spend extravagantly on luxuries for themselves. It is disheartening to see a man who owns a car worth lakh's but hesitates to give his wife even a small amount for her basic needs. A woman who nurtures her children, manages the household, and lives under his care should never feel abandoned in her financial rights.

Beyond financial neglect, another major cause of emotional and moral breakdown in marriages is the husband's lack of attention to his wife. Many men are consumed by their phones, social media, or work, failing to invest time in their marriages. This negligence not only affects the emotional and mental well-being of their wives but also deeply impacts their children. Islam emphasizes the importance of a husband fulfilling his wife's physical, emotional, and financial needs. The Prophet Muhammad (ﷺ) set the best example, saying:

"The best of you are those who are best to their wives, and I am the best among you to my wives." (Tirmidhi)

In my view, if every man, especially a Muslim man, acknowledges that just as **ALLAH (SWT)** has created him with a purpose, He has also brought a woman into existence with an equally significant purpose, then harmony and fulfillment will naturally follow. Men and women are meant to complement each other, forming the foundation of a meaningful and beautiful life together.

If every man approaches matters concerning women with patience, respect, and compassion—if he takes personal responsibility for upholding his wife's dignity, self-worth, and rightful entitlements—then the countless women who feel lost in the chaos of life will inevitably rediscover their existence with a renewed sense of purpose and fulfillment.

Moreover, another prevalent issue is the imbalance in how men treat their wives' families. While they expect their wives to respect, serve, and make endless sacrifices for their own parents and relatives, they often disregard their wives' families entirely. Islam, however, teaches fairness and justice in relationships. A righteous husband should show kindness and respect to his wife's family, just as he expects her to do the same for him.

Despite all these struggles, women must remember that if their suffering in marriage reaches an unbearable limit, Islam does not compel them to endure oppression indefinitely. **ALLAH (SWT)** has granted them the right to seek a dignified way out rather than falling into immoral relationships. The Prophet Muhammad (ﷺ) said:

"There is nothing more hateful to **ALLAH (SWT)** than divorce, but, if necessary, it is permitted." (Abu Dawood)

Women must understand that their ultimate reliance should be on Allah, not on any man. If they face hardships, they should seek Allah's guidance through prayer and patience rather than taking sinful paths. As **ALLAH (SWT)** says in the Qur'an:

"And whosoever fears **ALLAH (SWT)** and keeps his duty to Him, He will make a way for him to get out (from every difficulty)." (Qur'an 65:2)

The path of righteousness is never easy, but it is always rewarding. A woman who upholds her dignity and seeks Allah's help instead of resorting to infidelity will find peace and success in both this life and the Hereafter.

My message to every individual and every ruler across the world is this:

Recognize and restore the rightful place of women in society. Whether it is the right to inheritance and property, access to education, the freedom to make sound decisions about their own lives, or the strength to raise their voice against injustice—these are not privileges to be granted, but divine rights that must no longer be denied. It is the collective responsibility of both men and women to safeguard a woman's dignity, protect her emotional and physical wellbeing, and honor the purpose of her existence.

A woman's role is not confined to nurturing children or managing a household. Her life carries a far greater purpose—one that has been bestowed upon her by her Creator, a purpose no one can revoke or redefine. She has been honored by Allah, and her potential extends beyond the walls of her home into the very heart of society.

To those in positions of power: assist in the empowerment of women. Use your authority not to silence, but to amplify their voices. Stand against every form of abuse, injustice, and violation of their rights. If you have been entrusted with leadership, know that you will be held accountable on the Day of Judgment. Fulfill your moral and legal responsibilities today so that tomorrow no soul stands in silence over the crimes committed under your watch.

To every reader—whether male or female—know this:

Within these pages, you will find reflections of your own story. This book is not just a testimony of Muslim women—it is the untold narrative of every home, every struggle, and every act of silent resilience. You will find pieces of yourself between these lines, for this book speaks from the soul of humanity.

Let us close with the eternal words of Allah, who reminds us of purpose and accountability:

"Whoever does righteousness, whether male or female, while he is a believer—We will surely grant them a good life, and We will certainly reward them according to the best of what they used to do."

—Surah An-Nahl (16:97)

May this book be a voice for the unheard, a light for the veiled, and a step toward justice for all.

I have keenly observed and frequently noted that our society fails to grant women the respect and dignity they rightfully deserve. A woman is inherently entitled to protection, love, and compassion, yet many men perceive honoring and upholding her rights as an affront to their own superiority. This injustice becomes even more pronounced after marriage, where a husband's failure to acknowledge his wife's dignity and fulfill his obligations is often normalized.

Over time, this persistent disregard turns into a fate imposed upon women—one where humiliation and emotional neglect become their lifelong reality. As a result, their self-esteem is buried under the weight of unappreciation, leaving them devoid of identity and selfworth. In many cases, these wounds run so deep that a woman loses all sense of her individuality, forced to exist in a state of silent endurance.

There is a profound difference between truly living and merely existing. When a woman is stripped of her emotional security, her fundamental rights, and her personal identity, she becomes nothing more than a shadow of herself—a soul trapped in a life devoid of meaning. This silent suffering has tragically become the destiny of countless women in our society. My question is directed to every woman who hears my voice—how much longer will she accept humiliation as her destiny? For how long will she sacrifice her dignity at the altar of patience, allowing others to trample upon her selfrespect? If a woman remains unaware of her own worth even today, then when will she truly begin to live? And if her voice continues to be silenced, then in which era will she finally be granted the rights she inherently deserves as a human being?

I want to shed light on a deeply unsettling yet often ignored form of oppression—one inflicted by women upon each other. It is a harsh reality that, more often than not, a woman's greatest adversary is another woman. The cruelty, emotional torment, and relentless injustices women inflict upon one another are deeply alarming.

This oppression is most evident within in-law relationships, where women themselves become the enforcers of societal cruelty. It manifests in the ruthless mistreatment of stepdaughters by their stepmothers, the silent suffering of orphaned girls at the hands of their sisters-in-law, and the heartbreaking betrayals disguised as friendship.

Why is it that a woman cannot bear to see another woman happy? Why does the success of one become intolerable for another? Why is it that when a woman raises her voice for justice, those who silence her are often other women? Why do we, as women, stand against our own rights, becoming instruments of oppression rather than champions of support and solidarity?

As human beings, we are bound to make mistakes—this is part of our nature. However, what truly defines us is our ability to acknowledge our shortcomings and turn back to **ALLAH (SWT)** with sincerity. The Prophet Muhammad (ﷺ) beautifully emphasized this in his words:

"All the children of Adam are sinners, and the best among sinners are those who repent." (Sunan Ibn Majah 4251)

Allah, in His boundless wisdom, has honored humankind above all creation, granting us the status of Ashraful Makhluqat—the most dignified of beings. Unlike animals, we have been gifted with intellect, willpower, and the ability to differentiate between right and wrong. These qualities empower us to strive for continuous selfimprovement, not only in our deeds but in our connection with the Divine.

My message to everyone is simple yet profound: each day presents an opportunity to become a better version of ourselves. For every Muslim woman, repentance should not be limited to words alone but reflected in her actions—through the sincerity of her Salah, the refinement of her character, and the conscious effort to walk the path of righteousness. True beauty lies in strengthening one's bond with Allah, in seeking His mercy, and in living a life that brings us closer to Him.

May we all commit to self-improvement, seek His guidance, and embrace the journey of faith with unwavering devotion.

Through personal experience, I have realized that when a person—especially a woman—repents sincerely, calls upon her Lord with a devoted heart, and places complete trust in Him, she attains an unparalleled closeness to Allah. In such moments, she reaches a state of spiritual fortitude where neither worldly temptations can sway her nor external hardships can weaken her resolve. Instead, she emerges as unshakable as a mountain—strong, fearless, and self-sufficient. At this stage, she no longer seeks reliance on any worldly protector, for she discovers that her only true and eternal guardian is **ALLAH (SWT)** alone.

As I bring this book to its conclusion, my heartfelt message to all is this: we must never forget that there was a time when women were buried alive—denied even the most fundamental right to exist. It was then that Allah, in His infinite wisdom, brought Islam into being. Through the noble character and guidance of our beloved Prophet Muhammad (ﷺ), women were elevated from the depths of oppression and granted dignity, rights, and a place of honor in society, while men were liberated from the darkness of ignorance and cruelty.

What we now refer to as "women empowerment" was, in truth, introduced centuries ago through the light of Islam.

The pressing question we must ask ourselves today is this: why are those very rights—bestowed upon women not out of pity but because they are inherently deserving—not being upheld?

In my personal view, the foremost reason is ignorance and the erosion of faith.

We have become merely literate, not truly educated. We have reduced knowledge to academic degrees, superficial understanding, and impatience. We chase worldly accolades while drifting further from spiritual depth.

In many ways, we have turned ourselves into deities—disregarding the divine commands of **ALLAH (SWT)** and living as though we are accountable to no higher power.

If we genuinely desire to transform our circumstances, we must reshape our lives in accordance with the Sunnah of the Prophet Muhammad (ﷺ) and the divine commandments of Allah—the very guidance that restored a woman's dignity and rights, and rescued men from injustice by making paradise the reward for honoring women.

My final message to all is this:

Life and death have been created by our Lord with purpose and as a test, as explicitly mentioned in the opening verse of ***Surah AlMulk***:

"Blessed is He in whose hand is dominion, and He is over all things competent – ***[He] who created death and life to test you [as to] which of you is best in deed – and He is the Exalted in Might, the Forgiving."***

(Surah Al-Mulk, 67:1-2)

Therefore, our foremost duty is to fulfill the right of being a creation of the Creator. We must lead a purposeful life, for as believers, we are not at liberty to live like beasts—following desires without accountability. Even animals know how to eat, drink, and satisfy their physical urges. They too reproduce and raise their offspring. But **ALLAH (SWT)** has honored human beings as Ashraful Makhluqat—the most dignified of all creation.

A true believer must strive each day to live with greater intention and integrity. Each morning should begin with a renewed resolve—to distance oneself from sins, to rectify past errors, and to walk with sincerity on the path of righteousness so that we may live up to the high status granted to us by our Creator.

Man is not merely a body made of clay. Within us resides an eternal soul—one that was brought into existence long before the creation of Adam, in the realm of Ruh al-Arwah (the world of souls). Therefore, our primary effort should be devoted not to the fleeting needs of the body, but to the everlasting essence of our soul. The body is perishable, no matter how advanced we become. It is the soul that endures, and it is the soul that deserves our deepest care and attention.

Therefore, it is incumbent upon every man in this world to rise above the arrogance and ego that often accompany masculinity.

He must remember that the very reason for his existence lies in a woman—a woman who, despite enduring immense pain and hardship, gives him life. Before striving to be a man, one must first strive to become a true human being. Imagine, even for a moment, a world devoid of women—how bleak, lifeless, and unrecognizably barren it would become.

To every young woman of this era—especially my Muslim sisters—this is my heartfelt message:

ALLAH (SWT) has promised eternal paradise to His righteous servants—whether male or female—along with a life that will never fade.

"Whoever does righteousness, whether male or female, while being a believer – We will surely grant them a good life, and We will surely give them their reward [in the Hereafter] according to the best of what they used to do."

(Surah An-Nahl, 16:97)

So do not chase the noise of people; listen instead to the voice of your Lord. Do not seek validation, praise, or acceptance from the creation—seek to know your True Creator. Only when you draw near to your Lord will you begin to understand the true essence of your existence. **ALLAH (SWT)** has bestowed upon the righteous woman an elevated rank and a position of great honor.

If you are sincere, if you are honest with yourself—then there is no need to run after the fleeting approval of others.

Embrace patience and piety.

Value your self-worth.

Live with dignity, with your head held high—for only then will you fulfill the right of being a creation of Allah.

And when you live in accordance with the commands of your Lord and worship Him through your actions, only then can you raise a generation that is conscious, empowered, and guided.

The greatest form of arrogance is to deny the Word and Command of Allah.

So, listen to all but submit only to your Lord—for He alone governs the system of every era.

Do not be anxious about how to reshape divine guidance to fit the demands of a changing era. Rather, concern yourself with how to nurture yourself—and the generations to follow—so that they may adapt to every era with clarity, purpose, and unwavering connection to their true identity. Only then will they thrive not as imitators of the world, but as bearers of divine legacy.

As I reach the final pages of this book, my heart overflows with hope and sincerity. To every reader—man or woman—know that this is not just my story, but yours too. These words carry the silent struggles and quiet strengths found in every home. Within these chapters lie pieces of your mother, your sister, your wife, your daughter—and perhaps, even yourself. This book speaks of burdens carried behind smiles, of prayers whispered in the dark, and of strength clothed in silence.

My final message is this: may you rise above the noise of the world and come closer to the One who created you. May you honor your purpose, live with dignity, and never forget the value of your soul. Be a voice of compassion in a world that often forgets mercy.

And above all, know that your worth is not measured by society's standards, but by the light of your connection with your Creator.

"Indeed, those who have said, 'Our Lord is Allah' and then remained steadfast—angels will descend upon them, [saying], 'Do not fear and do not grieve but receive good tidings of Paradise, which you were promised.'"

(Surah Fussilat 41:30)

May **ALLAH (SWT)** guide our hearts, forgive our shortcomings, and make us among those who live with purpose and die with faith.

Ameen.

9 788199 324008

Printed at Repro India Ltd.